T0209757

"Drawing on Sean's experience as a youth pastor, *Youth Empowered* offers necessary insights and helpful suggestions for developing a thriving, student-led youth ministry that resonates with the needs of future generations. This book is a valuable contribution from an emerging, thoughtful leader in youth ministry."

Abdu Murray, Author and Speaker

"John Wesley noted that ministry is not the end of discipleship, but rather the means. Sean Buono has incorporated this dictum into a paradigm of teen ministry that is changing the landscape of youth work. Buono tailors his book on how to develop a student-led youth ministry of any size. If you are looking for a pathway to disciple your youth to become leaders in the church, this book is for you!

Dr. Matthew A. Lewis
Director for Practical Theology and Ministry
Brethren in Christ Church
Great Lakes Conference

"Sean Buono provides wisdom and insight for the church, which finds itself at a critical juncture in 2020: 'How do we reach the youth of today in order to develop our leaders for tomorrow?' *Youth Empowered* provides a theological framework for the biblical call to reach youth, then it lays out a relational approach to fulfill this mandate. Buono calls for a dynamic change in how ministry must shift in order to prepare our youth, as well as the church, for ministry in the 21st century. As a former lead pastor of a large church with 200+ active high school students in its youth ministry, I highly recommend this book to all youth ministers, youth leaders and lead pastors."

Reverend William M. Beachy, Ph.D.
Associate Professor of Pastoral Leadership and Spiritual Formation for Ashland Theological Seminary

"Sean Buono has lived this book! He gives theological insights, principles and practical methods to get students involved in the work of ministry. This resource will help youth leaders successfully facilitate a 'priesthood of all believers' among their young parishioners."

Pastor Kellen Brooks
Senior Pastor, Pentecostal Temple Church of God in Christ - Inkster, MI

"When Jesus called His disciples, He clearly trained them to do the work of ministry. Yet, many times in youth ministry, we simply *teach* students without *empowering* them. *Youth Empowered* is a much needed and timely work that will help any youth pastor learn how to empower their students for ministry. Sean Buono explains why it is important to teach youth to utilize their gifts for ministry and gives a practical, step-by-step approach to creating an environment that allows students to lead. By implementing the strategies found in this book, students in your youth ministry will learn how to engage their peers and effectively win souls to Christ."

Jesse Stirnemann
Youth Pastor, Victory Christian Church – Clinton Twp., MI

*Launching a Student-Led Youth Ministry
to Develop Church Leaders of Tomorrow*

SEAN BUONO

WESTBOW
PRESS®
A DIVISION OF THOMAS NELSON
& ZONDERVAN

WestBow Press books may be ordered through booksellers or by contacting:

WestBow Press
A Division of Thomas Nelson & Zondervan
1663 Liberty Drive
Bloomington, IN 47403
www.westbowpress.com
1 (866) 928-1240

Interior Image Credit: Sean Buono

ISBN: 978-1-9736-8167-0 (sc)
ISBN: 978-1-9736-8166-3 (e)

Print information available on the last page.

WestBow Press rev. date: 1/16/2020

For Kara. I am so very blessed to journey this life together with you. I love you, always and forever.

CONTENTS

Part 1

The Calling for a Student-Led Youth Ministry

CHAPTER 1

The World of Today's Youth Ministry

"The millennials are leaving the church in droves!"

In recent years, this statement is being heard at an increasing rate. While that claim sounds alarming, data shows that it is true now more than ever. The Pew Forum, a research center on religion and public life, has shown a steady decrease in the percentage of millennials affiliating with the Christian faith ever since the generation has become old enough to be recognized as its own age group. In the religious affiliation report, which was published in 2019, data showed that the percentage of millennials who have chosen to separate themselves from the Christian faith is higher than *all* of the other age groups—*combined*. Due to this rate of decline, which could take decades to turn around, youth ministry is quickly becoming one of the most pertinent ministries for churches to increase its focus on.

While such data appears to hint at doom and gloom for the future church, it does not have to be so; we can interpret it differently. We are shocked when our youth leave the church. However, do we stop patronizing a restaurant if we believe that its food is no longer enjoyable? Do we vote for a political candidate if we don't believe that they represent the values and needs that are important to our families? Perhaps the current youth exodus is not the death knell of the church. Instead, it is merely the voice of our youth speaking out. They are proclaiming their frustration toward a church that has—in their opinion—been unable to compete in the postmodern marketplace of ideas.

Nevertheless, we are encouraged to keep fighting the good fight. As believers in Jesus Christ, we can stand firm on two key convictions. First, the Christian faith is more relevant today than it has ever been. Second, our God is bigger than the secularization of the Western church. Thus, we must come to the table with a new approach for our youth. They are telling us—loud and clear—that what we have been doing for the past ten years is no longer working.

Undoubtedly, you have recognized these trends, as well. I applaud you for noticing the dire need for change during such a pivotal time in the church. You may have picked up this book because you are looking for a different youth ministry framework—one that is bold, attractive, winsome and effective. This book proposes that a student-led youth ministry satisfies this framework. The vision of a student-led youth ministry dares to imagine a youth ministry where the majority of its operations are handled by students. In a student-led youth ministry, the youth pastor and their fellow youth leaders guide and minister to the students from *among* the crowd, rather than *at* the crowd. Instead of applauding the occasional student who shows potential signs of full-time ministry in their future, a student-led youth ministry approaches the audacious concept that all youth can become actively involved in their church, in some form or fashion, at their current age. While we will certainly unpack all of the details surrounding this proposal, we must first tackle the concept of *why* student-led youth ministry is vital.

Going back to the '80s, much of student ministry has been events-based and focused on building friendships through programs. Since students didn't interact with a large number of other students outside of school and sports, youth ministry events-based programming helped fill the gap. However, in today's information age, the events-based student ministry that thrived in the '80s and '90s has quickly lost its appeal. Students are bored with a constant barrage of icebreakers and overnight lock-ins. While those things are not bad, students interact with a significantly larger number of peers on a daily basis due to social media. Today, there is no longer a need to attend an event at church in order to feel connected to peers. Slowly, the church is coming to the realization that events-based programming is no longer enough. We must accept the reality that the demands of today's youth ministry have vastly shifted away from what youth pastors once enjoyed and experienced during their formative years as a student.

We are now being called to build a ministry for tomorrow instead of reacting to the youth ministry needs of today. With the culture changing at such a rapid pace, the system must be scalable, adaptable and moldable on the fly. The days of church staff-powered ministry are quickly becoming extinct, and the new age of crowdsourcing-powered ministry is on the horizon. Indeed, we are now at a pivotal point in this shift of ministry mindset, where such a radical proposal will be met with large resistance from those who have been in ministry for decades. The former tried and true methods of staff-driven marketing, evangelism and teaching are all safe. It's a numbers game, after all, right? Preach to one hundred; baptize a few. Pay a few hundred dollars for some Twitter ads and Facebook ads; welcome a few new families. Tried. Tested. True. However, if only we could understand the power of the youth and the future landscape of ministry, these numbers would be realized as unsatisfyingly mediocre. The methods of 20th century youth ministry are now inadequate, and our current administrators and church leaders need to come to terms with the fact that we must change our youth ministry *in order to change our youth ministry.*

Perhaps it might benefit us first to ask what the purpose of youth ministry is. If the answer is to educate youth on the Word of God and encourage them to give their lives to Christ, then the church may be missing a key point. While such a response is certainly not wrong, it is lacking. Students today are hungry for truth. But it is not simply truth from a factual standpoint that they are seeking; it is a truth that must be conveyed through relational means. For now, let's call this "relational truth" (not to be confused with "relative truth"). In a world with an abundance of experts and technology, youth are not lacking access to information. Instead, they lack the level of relational connectivity from which the truthful information is derived.

Have you ever watched a teen speedily scroll through countless posts on their social media feed, only to abruptly stop to watch a video or read an article that seemed to be worthy of their time? Today's youth are astoundingly intuitive in identifying when something is relationally true. After all, they have to be! In their social media feeds of fake news, online ads, online bot-posts, and less-engaging content from some of their "friends," a student must have a knack for knowing when it's worth their time to stop and listen. Thus, when a youth pastor recites long strands of Scripture, or does another sermon series that has no relational connection to what they experience on a daily basis, the "tune out" button is immediately pressed in their minds and they, once again, wander off into daydream land.

But how can we successfully convey relational truth to our youth? Relationships take time. While icebreakers are great, their effectiveness is diminished if that is the only engagement that students have with others throughout a youth service. A retreat may be a phenomenal way to come together and build relationships, but these occur once—maybe twice—a year in most ministries. After the student returns from a retreat to their daily temptations, all of the relational truth that they received over a weekend is in danger of being undone. Some youth pastors may raise a concern about how they can consistently spend time with their students if they only see them once a week. Such a concern is valid, for the dilemma is that the church is in need of a system that encourages students to connect with God and their youth ministry more often than just one hour a week. There must be a way to make faith more tangible for our students seven days a week.

It is because of this dilemma that "the why" of today's youth ministry is realizing that the goal is more than just "getting them saved." In addition to the message of salvation, "the why" of today is evolving into an equipping of our youth in such a way that they not only understand their spiritual gifts, but that they also are consistently putting them to use for the benefit of the kingdom of God. Instead of feeding the students information on why they should give their lives to Christ, we provide relational guidance as to how they can change their world within the context of their relationship with Christ. It is through this collision of faith and life that the church is able to help the student understand what gift(s) the Lord has blessed them with, and perhaps even begin to shape the calling that the Lord has placed on their lives.

This methodology may be similar to the older models of program-based youth ministry, but there exists a subtle shift. Over the past ten years, our media consumption has moved away from the one-direction television programming toward an on-demand approach, where the user controls what to watch or listen to. Similarly, the church must also move away from one-direction programming or education and, instead, move toward a collaborative and engaging model of youth ministry that serves *alongside* the students. This model allows the youth to have a say in how they pursue ministry and their own spiritual growth.

Implementing a student-led youth ministry may sound extremely daunting. Your students' interest in youth service may not feel like it is at an adequate level in order to make this happen. Your supervisor who lived in the glory days of program-based youth ministry may scoff at such a preposterous concept. The parents of students in your group may raise an eyebrow when you hand a microphone to their student to have them share their testimony. However, this is to be expected. Before we become distracted by the naysayers and the skeptics, it is important to prayerfully consider that whenever we venture into unknown territory, there will always be uncertainty and a bit of fear. Even the Israelites experienced this when they were seeking the Promised Land. If it wasn't for a courageous few like Joshua and Caleb, who saw through the fear, perhaps it's possible that they may have wandered for another 40 years in the wilderness (Numbers 13:30-14:10). Be encouraged. Be a Joshua or a Caleb. Our youth of today don't have another 40 years to wander aimlessly.

CHAPTER 2

Laying the Foundation

While we may have addressed the question, "Why does our youth ministry exist?" we still need to tackle the bigger question at hand: "Why student-led youth ministry?" The answer to our question is multi-faceted, and it calls for us to first take inventory of the current state of today's youth culture by unpacking various elements.

Constantly Shifting Technology

Let's tackle the most obvious of what sets today's youth ministry apart from the former years of youth ministry: *technology*. The world is unarguably transforming the landscape of communication at lightning speed, and the youth are at the forefront of it all. Published books on how to create an effective student ministry used to have some sticking power for a few years. But now, due to its inability to address the challenges associated with social media and technology, we won't likely read past the cover of a youth ministry book if it was published before 2012. Social media began to take shape with mediums such as

AOL Instant Messenger, Myspace and Facebook from 2000 to 2004. However, the combination of Instagram's release in 2010, and the United States crossing the 50% saturation level of smartphones in 2012, is when youth truly began to incorporate social media into their daily communication and their overall identity.

Perhaps one of the biggest impacts of what social media has done for our youth is that it has given them a voice. Previously, one's reach of influence was limited to the social structures that were within the student's immediate environment (i.e., with their sports teams, their school friends, their family, etc.). Students were told what to do and think at school, at home, and even at church. Perhaps this used to be effective when the world's experts were highly vetted and fewer in numbers. But the influence that our church leaders used to have has suddenly become diluted in an information age where anyone can publish their opinion in a matter of minutes.

With social media, the entire world is now a potential audience. Anyone can now be considered a valued content creator. Don't forget that the highest paid YouTube streamer in 2018 was an eight-year-old child who reviewed toys. With such an even-level playing field, the youth have come to the realization that they are no longer just consumers of the world's information. They are also contributors. As a result, they increasingly view their world through the shared experiences of those around them. They also have a keen understanding of how they can impact others around them.

Our youth live in a globally-connected world today where interaction with anyone and everyone is a constant reality. If the Christian worldview is not adequately relevant or tangible, and if it doesn't give them the opportunity to interact with their world, pursuing a greater level of faith can possibly be dismissed from their list of the activities that are vying for their time. In other words, students today may stop attending youth ministry—not because they disagree with its principles or teachings—but because they may feel like there is a lack of connection due to its shortage of opportunities to fully engage. The truth is that our students today are more in control than ever when it comes to determining what they receive and what they can contribute. A church that refuses to acknowledge the reality of this is a church that shamefully underestimates the spiritual horsepower that a youth ministry can possess.

Are students' temptations and sins the same as they were years ago? Absolutely! We know from the Word of God that there's nothing new under the sun (Ecclesiastes 1:9). What is different today are simply the vehicles of sin that Satan is using. The speed and accessibility in which sinfulness is now available to our youth is unprecedented, and the challenges outlined in how to tackle these vehicles have never been previously known. Just as the devil has shifted his tactics to target our youth through different channels, the church must develop new strategies and channels, as well. It's time to recalibrate. Until we view youth ministry through the perspective of a student living in a technology-driven information world, we will be unable to understand how to connect with them and help address their spiritual needs within the context of their culture.

"What is Truth?"

In his book, *Saving Truth* (Zondervan, 2018), RZIM Senior Vice President Abdu Murray proposes the argument that we are now residing in a world known as a "post-truth" society, where the culture no longer respects the authority of truth if it runs counter to our feelings and preferences. In essence, the culture is now training our youth to disregard a moral absolute and instead adopt a stance that honors the desires of the self above the facts. Even if a student's actions are determined to be sinful in nature from a biblical standpoint, the authority of the Scriptures alone is not necessarily enough to inspire a student to change his or her ways. As a result, the challenge at hand is for the church to try to remain a reliable voice while competing with such a blatant disregard of moral authority.

Derived from G.K. Chesterton's teachings is the commonly known epigram, "When a man stops believing in God, he doesn't then believe in nothing. He believes anything." In the midst of the confusion and uncertainty of a post-truth culture that goads our youth into seeking out their fleshly desires, the temptation for a student to adopt a pluralistic view of truth becomes enticing. Without a firm Christian foundation to catch them in their fall, the student may develop a sense of confusion in not knowing what is good or evil.

Pontius Pilate asks the question in John 18:38, "What is truth?" Our youth may be asking this very same question, publicly or privately. As was previously mentioned, today's youth are hungry for relational truth. Relational truth is not just information and it's not just about relationship; it's a combination of the two. If they wanted to read the Bible, they would—it's on their phones. We can no longer simply explain to students why they should read their Bibles or why they should give their lives to Christ. Instead, students are looking for the answer to the question, "Why does Christianity matter to me and those around me in today's world?"

Living Today as a Teen

What the youth of today are going through is tough. The social landscape of today is different from anything we ever experienced growing up, and it's more unforgiving. Gone are the days of normal bullying. Here to stay is the haunting reality of cyberbullying, where it is said that more than half of teens have been a victim of it. Depending on the report that is referenced, the average age of a young person seeing pornography for the first time is beginning to trend toward the age of eleven. Studies also commonly show that the majority of teen boys in America are addicted to pornography. With the American Psychological Association sharing that the divorce rate is currently hovering between 40-50%, broken and blended families are now a natural part of the makeup of the church. As we scratch the surface, it becomes quite clear that a teenager is able to relate to adult problems more readily than we'd care to admit. In addition, it's becoming more likely that some of the very best individuals who can relate to students the most are their peers who they sit beside during service.

As mentioned earlier, many students are leaving the church when they go to college. We commonly hear these students say, "I don't believe Christianity is true anymore," or "My understanding of faith has evolved." The older generation may respond to this statement by providing even more sermons and telling their students that they simply need to read their Bible more. But it wasn't because of a few sermons missed along the way that millennials are arriving at these statements of unbelief. Rather, it's the lack of relational truth that is creating a void in our students' hearts. Were we to view their responses through the lens of relational truth instead, they become translated to mean something like, "I don't feel that Christianity is applicable to my life and what I am experiencing with those around me."

The Role of Youth Ministry

If the goal of today's youth ministry is to equip students to practice their faith in the context of developing a relationship with Christ, we must shift from the church's age-old models of sermon-focused and program-based youth ministry. Youth ministry is not merely another classroom; it is a training ground for students to understand how their faith can transform their world. Just as it is any parent's goal to properly train their child with sufficient life skills to survive on their own as an adult, a youth ministry should be able to confidently claim that its students are adequately prepared to serve in a ministry within the larger church.

There is a level of faith that is required before implementing a student-led youth ministry. Youth pastors will need to trust leaders and students to a degree that they may not be used to. By placing trust in more individuals, there is a chance that some will let us down. Students may forget to attend the youth ministry events. Youth leaders' schedules will inconveniently change at the last minute. Some may forget what they promised to do. It will take organization, planning and consistent communication. It will call you to put pride aside and take a fraction of the credit for the work you have done. Yet, by sharing the ministry with your students and your fellow youth leaders, God will be glorified in ways that you never would have expected. In addition, students will walk away with a greater level of confidence. Let us embark on this incredible journey of empowering others within the youth ministry. Let us believe and witness God do incredible things through our youth.

CHAPTER 3

Maintaining a Balanced Structure

In order to implement an effective student-led youth ministry, students must be trained effectively. However, in order for students to *want to* be trained, they must also have relationships in place to give them a backdrop for which their ministry efforts can be placed. While there is no precise recipe for the perfect implementation of a youth ministry, understanding the balance between relationships and serving can help greatly in knowing where your youth ministry stands today.

A visual called The Empowerment Chart can assist us in unpacking our proposed model of a student-led youth ministry. As seen in Figure 3.1, the X-axis of The Empowerment Chart represents the spectrum of student-based ministry. This will assist in determining the degree to which a youth ministry encourages their students to take ownership of the youth ministry's responsibilities. The left half of the chart shows the spectrum leaning toward the youth pastor assuming more responsibility, while the right half shows the spectrum leaning toward the students assuming more responsibility. The Empowerment Chart's Y-axis represents the degree in which the youth ministry pursues the development of relationships within its structure. The upper half of the chart shows the spectrum leaning toward the ministry adopting a structure that is more relational, while the bottom half of the chart shows the spectrum learning toward the ministry adopting a structure that is less relational.

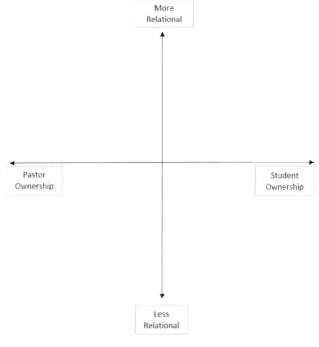

Figure 3.1

For the purpose of our model, The Empowerment Chart speaks to the representation of time spent *while* the youth ministry comes together during services and events. In other words, during any given youth service, how much time is dedicated to games, relationship building and fun activities? On the other hand, how much time is dedicated to training up your students in the faith so that they may be able to actively utilize their spiritual gifts and minister to others?

Should a youth ministry stray too much toward one of the farthest ends of The Empowerment Chart, instability is likely to occur. Thus, an effective student-led youth ministry becomes more challenging to implement as it moves farther away from the center point (see Figure 3.2). It is noteworthy to point out that Jesus modeled a perfect balance of these components. In the Scriptures, we see Him challenging us to love each other as He loves us (John 15:12), while also challenging us to go out and make disciples of the nations, spreading the good news and serving one another (Matthew 28:19; Matthew 22:39). To pursue too much of one, at the expense of the other, would show us to be in disobedience to the example that Jesus laid out for us.

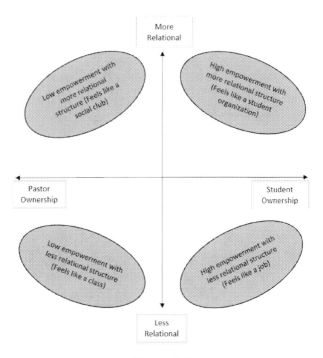

Figure 3.2

High Empowerment/High Relational

If the youth ministry encourages students to become involved in youth ministry opportunities, while driving a high level of relational involvement, the youth ministry ends up feeling like a collection of student organizations. Students may certainly be the working force of this type of ministry; however, under this model, they receive little mentorship as to how their ideas can be channeled into strategic spiritual growth. Besides the message that is preached, and any tasks that the youth pastor must accomplish, the youth are left to their own devices and are encouraged to build their own community through interest groups. The hope is that, in this scenario, a teen's experience in the youth ministry is fueled by their individual interests and they are given enough resources to create the type of youth ministry they most desire. Except for when assistance is required, gaming groups, hobby groups, Bible studies and other small groups are formed and maintained within the youth ministry without a consistently-engaged adviser. While this type of ministry helps students prepare for the freedom and leadership they will experience in college, a lack of mentorship in this model may cause the groups to lack depth and the youth ministry's overall vision may feel directionless. Under this model, students who subconsciously hunger for direction and accountability may lose interest quickly.

Low Empowerment/Low Relational

If the youth ministry refrains from inviting students to become involved in the youth ministry, while neglecting the relational needs of the students, the youth ministry ends up feeling like a class at school. Any relationship building that takes place is solely the responsibility of the students, and opportunities to connect among each other are rare. Valuing convenience more than discipleship, this type of model might take the form of a Sunday School that meets during the adult service. Here, the ability for the ministry to impact its students is contained within its ability to cram an entire service into a small amount of time. Students arrive to greet each other, hear announcements, listen to a message, and immediately leave to meet up with the parent, who is awkwardly standing by the door (because the youth pastor had the audacity to preach for an extra five minutes that morning). While this model may address the spiritual formation of the student body, the time that is required to allow organic relationships to grow is woefully lacking. Got a juicy topic where students need to be vulnerable? Sorry, we've run out of time and everyone has to go home. If the youth service takes place during the middle of adult service, then the vision and the goals of the youth ministry become subservient to the restrictions placed upon them by the adult ministry. While this is the logical starting point for a church plant, or a youth ministry that is starting from scratch, its restrictions outweigh its benefits in the long run. Understandably so, a youth ministry that is growing quickly realizes the need to break free from this model in order to accommodate and work alongside the movement of the Lord.

High Empowerment/Low Relational

If the youth ministry sets an expectation for its students to be involved in the youth ministry, while neglecting the relational needs of its students, participation in the youth ministry ends up feeling like a job. Such an environment assigns students to take a part in the ministry, whether it fits the students' spiritual strengths or not. Ministry is done because it has to be, and the church must pull together in order to make it happen. More commonly found in church plants, or communities where there exists a larger number of practical needs, this model values completion of the task more than the development of the individual.

With the needs of the community being so pressing, it becomes difficult to shift to a more balanced model due to the risk of leaving behind an essential ministry task. Students who graduate high school out of this youth ministry model may gain an understanding of what it means to put action to faith; however, they enter college with a lack of understanding of who they are and how their specific gifts can be used for the kingdom of God. At best, a student leaves high school with fond memories of serving in the youth ministry and they will remain encouraged to serve in some capacity once again in the future. At worst, a student experiences burnout and becomes bitter after being involved with too many ministry opportunities that were not aligned with their spiritual giftings.

Such a ministry develops a certain obedience to the concept of serving within the church, which, in itself, is not a bad thing. Yet, in today's post-modern culture, we are seeing proof that obedience alone is no longer sufficient in calling the youth to take ownership of their faith. Without engaging the heart of the student, and helping them understand who they were uniquely created to be, the church ends up being one of many options where they can do nice things for others, rather than a community where God transforms their lives and the lives of those around them.

Low Empowerment/High Relational

If the youth ministry lacks in its empowerment of students, while maintaining a high level of social involvement, the youth ministry ends up feeling like a social club. Perhaps the most common model found in youth ministry today, students know their youth ministry as a place to make friends and play games. Rather than being funneled through an overarching strategy of spiritual growth, messages are delivered at a surface level to address the common topics of teen years.

In this scenario, church staff usually believe that well-built relationships become the driving force for transformation in a teenager's life. The hope is that, in this scenario, a teen's experience of close friendships will inspire them to stay connected and warmly welcome them into service opportunities through the gravitational pull of positive peer pressure. While the intent of the staff is good, this type of youth ministry may take on a, "Let's see what sticks" strategy, which lacks structure for students to grow in ministry. If the staff's only focus is to foster an environment where students feel welcomed and comfortable, then today's youth will see this model as an attempt to entertain them.

While this is not a bad thing in itself, students end up recalling very little of their experience of youth ministry when they go off to college and are confronted by the pressures and temptations of the world. Through this model, the church teaches its students to become good friends rather than training them up to be disciples, thereby allowing the youth ministry to selfishly puff up its own numbers by marketing itself as a fun place to be. While the ministry looks relatively healthy from the outside, the long-term effects of this model end up harming the church. Indeed, these are the churches that are confused as to why so many of their students are leaving. They fail to realize that the severe underequipping of their students never allowed their youth to successfully take ownership of their own faith.

The impact of these less-balanced youth ministry models can affect the church in different ways. For instance, forced relationship or involvement do not sit well with today's youth. Today's students have enough going on; they certainly have no time or emotional tolerance to be forced into doing something that does not appear to benefit them. Because these more extreme models drive students away at a faster pace, the "job" and "student organization" types may be found less often within the world of youth ministry. On the other end of the spectrum, the "classroom" and "social club" youth ministry models will generate more of a silent discontent instead of a speedy exodus. Such models may be considered safer since they present a lack of pressure or a lack of commitment for the students.

Of these four, the latter two models promise the students that there is no risk to attend. They entice students to join with pandering programs or momentous events. They're hesitant to challenge students to work out their faith for fear of scaring them away. It's best to just be good buddies with them and cover the essential Bible verses so that, hopefully, they'll pick up enough to keep them interested and engaged until they graduate. While these models aren't intimidating, they are at least tolerable. Students don't mind obliging their parents to attend youth ministries with these models because at least they won't have to do something that they don't feel like doing (and perhaps there are a few friends from school to make it seem interesting). Unfortunately, these two models are hard to criticize since it is difficult to make the connection between the practicing of these models with the slow drain of youth numbers from the church. Nevertheless, there is a better way.

The Balanced Model

If youth are given an environment that provides a healthy balance between the relational and the empowerment components, this results in a true student-led youth ministry (as seen in Figure 3.3). Under a balanced model, students will naturally build relationships with their peers as they pursue ministry opportunities together. Students are granted a safe environment through which they can work out their faith and discover their spiritual gifts; students take ownership of their faith without feeling forced to; and students receive mentorship that will guide them to become actively engaged Christians, post-high school and beyond.

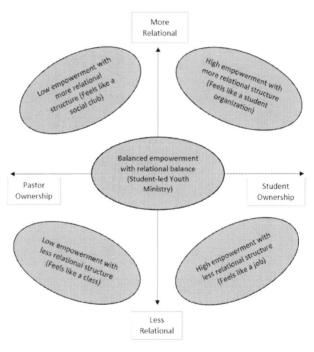

Figure 3.3

Implementation of a balanced model hinges on a few key factors, including the youth pastor's willingness to share leadership within the youth ministry; the support of church staff; and church resources that are available to the youth pastor. Without the youth pastor being open to sharing their leadership, decisions will end up being made hastily, less individuals will feel involved, and the youth pastor will have to do more work. Without the support of church staff, the youth pastor will fight an uphill battle that may encounter more road blocks caused by individuals who are insistent on pursuing youth ministry like the last thirty years. Without resources being made available for the youth pastor, critical components like a dedicated meeting space or a consistent meeting time, can prevent a balanced model from being launched without the extensive reworking of church resources at the highest levels. Should the key factors be properly in place, then faith, patience, time and prayer will all contribute toward the successful formation of a balanced student-led youth ministry model.

Part 2

The Make-Up of a Student-Led Youth Ministry

CHAPTER 4

The Current Profile of Your Youth Ministry

While there may be initial concerns for those who are considering a student-led youth ministry, one must not predict the level of success that they may have based on their youth ministry's current profile. For the youth pastor who is concerned with the idea that a student-led youth ministry will involve a large amount of extra work, fear not. It is worth noting that a student-led youth ministry will demand less of you, especially as time progresses. While there will be additional communication and planning involved as you combine the calendars of more individuals, the number of tasks on your plate will gradually decrease. As a result, you'll have more time to strategize and focus on the items on your list that only you can do (and should be doing).

For the youth pastor who is concerned that their students will not do well enough, keep the long-term goal in mind. Let us not forget that we, too, messed up when we first started in ministry. Students will make mistakes. They may say something that is not quite biblical by accident. They may embarrass themselves. They may even drop the ball and completely forget to do something for the church. We must not get hung up in the types of personalities that our students currently have. Instead, we must see our students for who God sees them and who they *are yet to become*. If your students are not exhibiting signs of leadership or passion for ministry, this might be due to the possibility that they have not been given the opportunities that truly tap into their spiritual giftings. Right from the onset, let's see the best in our students and create an environment that feels safe enough for them to make mistakes. We must not sacrifice opportunity at the altar of perfection if we are to properly build up our youth's church of tomorrow.

For the youth pastor who fears that their students will not want to participate, be encouraged. While change may not be comfortable for some students, progress can be made in small increments. Casting vision and framing a youth ministry's goals takes time. You can set your own timeline for the first phase of your student-led youth ministry. The goal would not be to force anyone into a ministry opportunity, but rather to locate where God is already moving within the youth ministry. Then, become the bridge that connects that individual to the ministry opportunity.

The culture of each youth ministry can vary from church to church. Opportunities that can be pursued in one church cannot be pursued in the others due to its number of active students. For the remainder of this book, a small-sized youth ministry will be considered to consist of two to twenty students. A medium-sized youth ministry will be considered to consist of twenty to fifty students, and a large-sized youth ministry will be considered to consist of fifty or more students. While it is typical that a church's youth ministry will generally correlate to the overall size of the church, there are cases where medium to large-sized churches have small-sized youth programs. If encountered, this particular scenario may raise attention to the strategies that the adult church may be utilizing to engage their students and help them feel involved within the walls of their community.

Each size of a youth ministry has different dynamics within the context of a student-led youth ministry. In a small program, the youth pastor is typically the only individual leading the group, although it is possible for one or two lay youth leaders to work alongside the youth pastor. Due to the size of this youth program, it operates quite similarly to how a co-ed small group would function. The group would most likely gather in an intimate setting and cater their activities and conversations to the specific interests of its individuals.

As the youth ministry grows to the size of a medium group, this is when things begin to pick up and the youth pastor will need assistance from the lay leaders. The youth group will begin to feel more church-like as worship songs and a sermon begin to be consistently included. Since there are enough students, small groups may be able to break out by gender now. The lay youth leaders develop close connections with the individual students (instead of it only being the youth pastor). Lastly, at the level of a large youth group, systems are put into place to let the youth program run very similar to the main adult church. Worship and teaching is much more structured, and separation by both gender and age within small groups is typically needed in order to keep the group sizes manageable.

We will address the needs of a student-led youth ministry within the context of each of these three sizes. True, there will be some overlap between the needs of these three sizes. But the number of differences between the systems are large enough to justify the need to address each one separately. To help us address each size of the program, we'll also analyze four specific areas that can impact the organization and structure of a student-led youth ministry: the youth pastor, the lay youth leaders, the students and the parents.

CHAPTER 5

Youth Pastor, Not Supervisor

The role of the youth pastor is the most crucial role in the entire vision of a student-led youth ministry. It is slightly ironic to make such a claim since the goal of a student-led youth ministry is to get the youth pastor out of the way and allow students to come forward. The youth pastor is the most crucial role because they are the one who sets the tone, the direction and the level of confidence for the path that lies ahead. They foster an environment where others feel comfortable to not only speak up and share ideas, but also to contribute and take ownership of any needs that come up. They uplift, inspire, motivate and empower. But what's most crucial is the need for the youth pastor to communicate that they are all in. Students and other youth leaders can sense when someone is genuine. The level of trust and empowerment that the youth pastor extends to their fellow leaders, and the students, will be easily recognizable. If the youth pastor has one foot in the old model, and one foot in the new model, they will be unable to hide it.

A large part of conveying this will be in the youth pastor's vision casting. While some pastors may have more of a natural gift of vision casting, every leader needs to do it. Whatever the vision is for your church—especially for your youth ministry—share it often enough so that anyone would be able to recite the vision when prompted. When committing to the advancement of a student-led youth ministry, share with your students and lay leaders what it would look like for them to be on stage leading worship, preaching sermons, greeting other students at the door and organizing service events. These images won't pop into their heads automatically. The devil won't allow that. God has called you to be a pioneer in your ministry. Do something radical and empower those who have never known or realized what they could do in ministry. You have been blessed with an image of what your youth ministry could look like and it's vital for you to share it on a regular basis.

But besides vision casting, the role of the youth pastor might be easier to define by determining what a youth pastor is *not*. First, the youth pastor is not a mini head pastor. Traditionally, the youth pastor's role has not ever been much of a glamorous job. They get pied in the face. They stay up all night at lock-ins. They plan ridiculously complex retreats (oftentimes singlehandedly), and they're expected to serve a population of youth who can be pessimistic, apathetic, and sometimes even cynical. The position is sometimes seen as a stepping stone to greener pastures, and the support offered from the church's senior leadership is not always sympathetic to the youth pastor's cause. If you are trying to act like your church's senior pastor, and you expect the honor and respect that he or she receives because of their position, stop. Position itself may grant authority and respect in the adult church;

however, this cannot be assumed with today's youth. To them, respect is earned on a daily basis.

Second, the role of youth pastor should no longer be considered an introductory position in ministry. What if the role did away with all of the stereotypical assumptions and replaced them with the concept that the youth pastor is raising up the church's future leaders? The overnight lock-ins and retreats will still be a part of the youth ministry. However, these activities would no longer be what *defines* the role of the youth pastor. Instead of the attitude that the youth pastor is simply babysitting a pack of wild students, what if the youth pastor's role was considered as highly esteemed as the other pastor(s) of the church? If such a thought might be considered ridiculous in your church, it might indicate how important it should be to pause and ask if your church's youth ministry is truly a piece of the entire vision of the church. Or, is it just the "other" ministry that takes place in the next room because some parents want their teens to be occupied for a few hours?

This may come across as harsh; however, the youth ministry is of equal importance to the children's ministry and adult ministry of your church. If the church supports one or two of these three ministries more than the other(s), then an imbalance will occur and people will drop off somewhere along the way. Some churches place a heavy emphasis on advancing its children's ministry to get the parents in the door. But if the staff puts very little focus on its youth ministry, teens will likely come to the conclusion that their emotional and spiritual struggles are not validated by the church. Perhaps teens leave the church to find other avenues that appear to be more validating of their identity and struggles. However, the shame here is that they find out too late that the world is unable to offer them anything better. As a result, the same parents we enticed with a stellar children's ministry may end up experiencing a series of familial spiritual struggles 10 to 15 years later due to the church's mediocre efforts of advancing their teens' spiritual development.

While your role as the youth pastor may be just as important as the children's pastor and senior pastor, it is important to note that it would not mean that each of your roles are the same. One of the goals of a children's pastor is to help young children get to know who Jesus is and that He loves them. While this particular spiritual principle is certainly supported and enacted throughout your youth ministry, it does not mean that it should be your youth ministry's main goal. If it is, then it is time to stop babying your students. They have seen and experienced enough of this world to know that they are no longer in need to be fed "book report" summary sermons on the Bible. They are ready for the real stuff. They are ready to digest the meat of the Word of God and determine what it means to apply it to their everyday lives. You can talk about drugs, sex, cyberbullying, suicide, pornography, abortion, cutting, gossip and everything in between. If you don't, the world will. More than likely, their friends are quite outspoken on these matters. In my experience of working with 7th and 8th graders, even these students are ready to join in on the conversation. After all, they are already looking up these topics online on their smartphones.

Likewise, one of the goals of adult ministry is to help make connections within the church membership and engage in small groups. While this particular spiritual principle is also supported and enacted throughout youth ministry, it does not mean that it should be your youth ministry's main goal. Adults are consumed with the busyness of life and they sometimes find it difficult to make meaningful connections within the church due to their schedules. Thus, *they* need encouragement and prompting to get together and make new friends. *Teens*, on the other hand, are already engaging with one another on a regular basis in the classroom, on the sports team and online. While fun games and social events are all certainly nice to have for the youth, we must determine if this truly is the area with the largest potential growth in our students' lives. If students are not struggling to make friends, or struggling to interact with one another, this would not need to be a primary focus of the youth ministry.

Welcoming the Input of Others

Although training and mentoring will always be a component of your role as youth pastor, *how* you mentor and train others will take on a different look and feel as your youth ministry grows. When a youth ministry is small, decisions can be made quickly and the youth pastor is typically the only voice of authority. Oftentimes, everyone looks to you and they have no problem following your lead. However, as the ministry grows, planning and collaboration with others becomes a requirement in order to help you stay on track. Just as the main church staff members have meetings with executive teams and/or the board of trustees, you as a youth pastor will need to adopt a similar system and meet with key leaders in your organization that you trust. Just as Jesus had three disciples in His inner circle that He pulled from the twelve, you, too, need to work alongside two to five sold-out leaders whom you feel can help you lead the organization. While there would not be a specific frequency to meet under, this "core planning group" of leaders should meet at least once a month to ensure that the ministry is on track with its mission and to make any changes, where necessary.

Student feedback in the leadership and planning process of youth ministry is also a key component. With technology and culture constantly shifting at lightning-fast speed, the experts who know best what students are struggling with are oftentimes the students themselves. A youth pastor who seeks no input from students is a youth pastor who is mistakenly out of touch. The day that they stop listening to what the students are saying is the day that their youth ministry becomes irrelevant. It's important to note that we should not roll over and do everything the students want or suggest. Instead, it's an earnest effort to hear what is going on in their lives and to pray through what they are suggesting. Students have spiritual gifts, too. For church leadership to dismiss what's on their hearts is unfortunate and detrimental to the spiritual growth of its students.

While methods of soliciting feedback within the setting of a small-sized youth ministry can be conducted more subtly (like during games with the youth or talking in the car during fast-food runs), your task of acquiring a pulse on the student body will need to adopt more structure as the size of your ministry increases. Perhaps in a medium-sized youth ministry, you might ask for your lay leaders to engage to find out what the emotional and spiritual needs of their respective students are. In a large youth ministry setting, you may even summon a quarterly student leadership team that helps your monthly core planning group in understanding the current challenges of the youth (more detail on this is found within chapters nine and ten, which cover Empower Teams).

In either scenario of leader collaboration or student collaboration, a student-led youth ministry will challenge the youth pastor to refrain from taking a supervisory type of approach to their ministry. Just as the senior pastor collaborates with other board members and lay leaders to make large decisions for the entire church body, the youth pastor could also benefit from adopting a similar approach. The larger the youth ministry, the more the youth pastor will require buy-in on any major changes within the context of a student-led youth ministry.

When I was youth pastoring at my church and we were shifting the meeting day and time of youth service, there was initially a severe pushback from both students and leaders. After talking through hours of meetings with key leaders and walking them through the reasons as to why this was occurring, a shift in the interpretation of the change took place. What started out as an outright refusal evolved into an excitement and full buy-in from the key leaders. These individuals then proceeded to take the message and the same enthusiasm to the students and the other leaders on the team. Eventually, the entire youth ministry was on board.

I could have put my foot down and said, "This is the way it's going to be!" I could have said, "I don't have time to try to convince these leaders. They just need to listen to me because I know the Lord called me to do this." But I didn't. As a result, both the leaders and the students took ownership of the change in the very best way possible. Of course, we all know that scenarios like these don't play out as smoothly as this one did. However, when including your fellow leaders in the decision-making process, you and your team of leaders will be able to successfully resolve disagreements and come to a mutually agreeable plan of action for the greater benefit of the youth ministry.

Youth Pastoring, According to the Size of Your Youth Ministry

For small youth ministries that are making an effort to evolve into a student-led youth ministry, the youth pastor's role involves more vision casting than youth pastors of larger-sized groups. If there are fewer students in the youth ministry, there are fewer roles and opportunities to serve as a student. While a youth ministry isn't necessarily comparable to a church plant regarding finances and property management, there certainly are some similarities in many of the other areas.

Any person who has been involved in a church plant would agree that it would be crucial to ask for the participation and involvement of those charter members who are there at the start. If the senior pastor constantly casts the vision, and empowers the charter members of a church plant, why wouldn't a youth pastor do the same with their initial students? To help create the groundwork of a full-fledged student-led youth ministry, the youth pastor in this scenario should build up their current students and groom them into future youth leaders of the ministry as the youth program increases to a medium size.

For medium-sized youth ministries that are exhibiting signs of a student-led youth ministry, the youth pastor's focus shifts from primarily vision casting to team building. While it was easier to do things spontaneously with a handful of students, trying the same things won't yield as much success when you have twenty or more students attending regularly. No longer can the group take up a corner of the local coffee shop or go on an impromptu road trip to the nearest amusement park, without leaving someone out. A need for organization and planning will naturally begin to arise, and the youth pastor will begin to lean on the assistance of lay leaders to help develop deeper connections with their students.

For some youth pastors, a "list" may be an evil four-letter word, but it is absolutely necessary. How will you remember to pray for that student, call that other lay leader on Wednesday, provide a progress report to your supervisor by Thursday, send out the parent email by Friday, and then coordinate with five different calendars on the next agreed monthly meeting time? Your superpower may have been remembering everything when your youth ministry was small, but students and parents become less forgiving when you, of all people, are not accountable to others.

For large-sized youth ministries that have the resources to fully adopt a student-led youth ministry, the youth pastor becomes a behind-the-scenes figure. He or she mentors other mentors within the youth ministry. Rarely does a youth pastor take credit for anything that's done, even if they are the ones who actually did the work. They become expert schedulers and they typically have roughly the next three to four months of the youth ministry's calendar planned out.

As the youth pastor may not have the opportunity to spend as much time making connections with individual students, they instead have an excellent handle on relationships with their lay leaders. By leveraging the power of decentralization, the youth pastor in this circumstance will be able to have the flexibility to address impromptu ministry needs, while your lay leaders continue to keep the machine well-oiled. Additionally, at this stage, it becomes helpful for the youth leaders to become the primary contact between the parents and the youth pastor. As a result, the main role of a youth pastor in a large student-led youth ministry is to be the biggest cheerleader on the team, the person who constantly makes connections and deeply cares about the outward expression of everyone's spiritual gifts.

CHAPTER 6

Youth Leaders, Not Employees

Youth leaders are truly a gift from the Lord. As the needs of a youth ministry increase, it becomes quite clear that the youth pastor is not able to do everything alone. The support of volunteer lay leaders is needed. But these volunteers are a unique group of people. Since they are not paid staff, youth pastors are unable to demand a level of follow-through that is enforceable. After all, they're volunteers; they can leave as quickly as they came. Yet, they also cannot be grouped together with the students since they have a few characteristics that the students don't have. For starters, they are outside of the target age range of the youth ministry. They also have a decent awareness of their spiritual gifts. Finally, they have received a call from the Lord to join your ministry and positively impact teens' lives alongside you.

But what role does a youth leader hold in your church? Are they there simply to help oversee one of the fun games that your group is playing that day? Are they there just to help facilitate conversations after the teaching? Or are they small group leaders who take on the calling to develop deeper connections with their students during the remainder of the week, outside of the church? While there's no secret formula for what youth leaders are supposed to be, it might be helpful for us to establish what youth leaders are *not*.

First, it is critical to emphasize is that your youth leaders are not youth pastors. Therefore, expectations surrounding the two roles should not be the same. Youth leaders need to be ministered to, just like the students in your youth ministry. One of the frustrations that youth pastors may encounter is that youth leaders are not independently pursuing their own faith to the degree that a pastor would expect from a lay leader within the church. Some youth leaders are fresh out of high school themselves, and their heart for the Lord naturally drew them back to the place where they felt most comfortable through the span of their high school career. We must respect the likelihood that some of the leaders on our team are working through a faith that is still maturing, young or old.

Youth pastors are called to not only serve and minister to students, but also to serve and minister to the very teammates who are working alongside them. This means that the one-on-one conversations, meals, social nights, late night phone calls, and everything in between are all a part of the package deal. This is no different from adult church, where the senior pastor has the same perspective for pouring into the lay leaders of the larger church through supplemental trainings and meetings. If tension is building up between the youth pastor and the youth leaders, it might be linked to a misaligned expectation that the youth pastor is holding over their youth leaders' spiritual growth. The sooner you stop expecting your leaders to be at the same level of spiritual growth as you, the sooner you will be able to better appreciate the service they bring to the youth ministry.

Some youth pastors that read this may be doubtful, thinking that there just isn't enough time in the day to serve both students and leaders at this level of involvement. The good news is that they're right. The reason why a youth pastor might think that this system won't work is because they're operating off an old model of youth ministry, where the youth pastor would roll up their sleeves and do it all. There isn't enough time. Trying to take on both of the groups will only increase the likelihood of burnout. In a medium to large-sized youth ministry, the youth pastor instead establishes connections with the youth leaders, while the youth leaders are the ones who are establishing the connections with the students. It's not that the youth pastor is not qualified to make connections with students; instead, it should be viewed in a light that offers to share the ministry load between more individuals on the team. If a youth pastor invites a youth leader to be a part of the team, but then makes it a habit to drop in to their small group and hijack their group conversations, or goes around the youth leader to mentor their students without the leader's knowledge, they may leave the youth leader wondering why they joined the youth ministry in the first place. The youth pastor has enough to do. Neglecting to give youth leaders enough trust and space to minister to their students undermines the calling that the Lord has placed on their lives.

Second, your youth leaders are not mind readers. They won't know what you want them to do unless it's communicated. As a youth pastor, clear and consistent communication is one of the most important tasks you can maintain for your youth leaders. Even though they may not be involved with church staff meetings, the decisions made at those staff meetings impact the direction of the youth ministry. While some decisions made within the walls of these staff meetings must stay private, a portion of them are worth sharing. These decisions help shed light onto how the youth ministry fits into the greater mission of the church. Similarly, while some youth leaders are not included in the core planning team meetings that you hold once a month with select leaders, almost all decisions made at those meetings should be shared with the greater team of your youth leaders.

Transparency is vital. Your youth group leaders act as an extension of the youth ministry's voice and mission. If your leaders are not included in the mission of the youth ministry, your students' spiritual growth could be negatively impacted, either by the grumbling of your youth leaders or the silence of your youth leaders. When I served as a youth pastor, I was extremely transparent. Youth leaders frequently voiced their opinions and asked questions about the direction of the student ministry. The conversations were collaborative and productive. Each time we got together, our unity as a team grew stronger and more pronounced.

Third, your youth group leaders may not have the same spiritual gifts as you. Similar to the first point, your youth leaders may not be as active in pursuing their faith and relationship with Christ. Similar to the second point, your youth leaders won't inherently know how to function in ministry like you do. However, this third point goes a bit further. Although the youth pastor is called to serve as a paid staff member for the church, they are not going to do everything perfectly.

As a youth pastor, you may be a stellar teacher. But if you are unable to be enthusiastic enough to carry the energy levels needed for making youth service fun and upbeat, it would be crucial for you to pass this ministry opportunity along to someone else who is gifted in this regard (or multiple individuals). Allow them to kick off the services, run the games and help plan the fun social events that occur outside of regularly scheduled services. Similarly, if instead of teaching, you have a gifting to build one-on-one relationships, it would behoove you and the youth ministry to invite more leaders and youth speakers up to the pulpit who have a passion and a gift for teaching. This isn't ducking out of your job duties. While many of us may have the stamina to run a few miles, we most certainly wouldn't dare represent the USA as a runner at the next Summer Olympics! If someone can do something better than you, and can represent the kingdom of God when key ministry opportunities arise, why not have the very best results possible?

It's important to be humble enough as a leader to put pride aside and acknowledge that you have blind spots. It's even better to be able to identify your blind spots so that you know when to look out for them. On any given day on the road, when changing lanes on the expressway, I first check my blind spot to make sure that I won't be in danger of crashing into anyone. In other words, I know those blind spots are always there, but it is most important to check them when I'm changing lanes. Similarly, in ministry, when planning a youth service or future sermon series, it helps to be able to check your blind spot(s) by involving those around you who have a better vantage point for the ministry needs at hand. The bigger the magnitude of the task at hand, the more time you should take to pause and consult your blind spots by involving others.

Finally, even though your youth leaders expect to be involved in the youth ministry, they are not your employees. The difference is subtle, yet transforming if understood fully. Should the youth pastor lack the ability to plan ahead, they develop a reactionary posture to ministry. This posture orders their youth leaders around instead of adopting a proactive stance, which offers their leaders an opportunity to serve in advance. Something as simple as a lock-in could appear quite chaotic if leaders arrive at the event to find that itineraries have not been printed out, or that the youth pastor is asking the team to fill in gaps that could have been prevented if tasks were properly planned in advance. This type of treatment of youth leaders can only occur so many times before volunteers begin to be "out of town" or "working" coincidentally on the evenings of future events.

Refusing to adequately prepare for your event unfortunately does not allow it to be more "Spirit-led." When events are properly planned, it creates a framework through which you and your leaders can expect to see the movement of God. This gives the Holy Spirit permission to arrive on the scene, assisting you and your leaders in ministering to your students.

Youth Leaders, According to the Size of Your Youth Ministry

For small-sized youth programs that are making an effort to evolve into student-led youth ministries, the youth leader's role may be a bit less involved than youth ministries of larger sizes. At the very least, the youth leaders who are on the team would assist with any small group discussions and events that take place for the ministry. Additionally, they would be natural candidates for your core planning team that meets once a month. More than likely, there may only be one or two youth leaders needed for a small youth ministry, and the youth pastor might be doing most of the work. He or she may be the only person building relationships with the students. However, this does not need to be the case. If you have a few youth leaders who are accountable and eager to take on a more active role within the youth ministry, there's no stopping a youth pastor from empowering the leader(s) to take full ownership of their role as mentor to the students.

For medium-sized youth programs under a student-led youth ministry, the need for youth leaders starts to become more prominent. This is the state of youth ministry where there may be enough students to break apart groups by gender; however, there may not be enough to break apart the groups also by age. Because of this, it's possible for youth leaders to tag team in mentoring students and/or facilitating small group discussions. This stage becomes a key season to begin practicing your organization and communication skills as a youth pastor. If you are able to keep your leaders informed and involved at this stage of the ministry, you will be adequately preparing your team for a future state of a large-sized youth ministry.

For large youth programs that have the resources to fully adopt a student-led youth ministry, youth leaders are an absolute must-have. At this size, groups should be able to be separated by both gender and age if the ministry has enough leaders to accommodate this format. While this particular recommendation would not make or break the possibility of success for a student-led youth ministry, there are three reasons why this format is optimal for a student-led youth ministry.

First, there is a certain level of intimacy that is achieved when a student can trust and confide in one consistent leader. In a season of their lives that is already full of changes, turmoil and cultural pressures, to be transparent with more than one adult might be more than a teen would care to invest in. Additionally, deeper connections with one leader means a better understanding of who each student is and what their spiritual gifts are. At my church, our leaders are given the opportunity to stay with their students from year to year. I had the honor and pleasure of walking alongside my group of guys for all four years of their high school careers, and I wouldn't have had it any other way.

Second, groups can stay small enough that a student can feel like they have a voice. Students may be coming from environments that do not allow them to have a voice (school, home, jobs, etc.), and a small group might be the last bastion of hope where a troubled teen can feel like they can share what's on their heart. If too many students are in a group, oftentimes we can miss those magical moments of a small group where the person who rarely speaks can feel comfortable enough to come forward and contribute.

Third, as your student-led youth ministry grows, you'll need to develop ministry teams that will resemble some of the ministries that are seen within the adult church. Increasing the number of leaders at this stage can help bring enough individuals to help lead these Empower Teams, when such teams are ready to launch. (See chapter nine and chapter ten for more information on Empower Teams and launching them.)

It would be important to note that as the number of leaders increase, and as the diversity of spiritual gifts increases within the team, the amount of responsibility that is shifted away from the youth pastor's workload should increase, as well. Otherwise, if a youth ministry is padded with leaders who are not really needed, leaders will begin disengaging when they realize that they can be more effective elsewhere within the church. Scheduling quarterly or semi-annual team-wide meetings that bring all leaders together can help prevent this. Also, regularly speaking with your leaders on a one-on-one basis can assist in understanding how your leaders are finding themselves within the youth ministry.

Having a dependable team of youth leaders can be the difference between a youth ministry that causes burnout and a ministry that blesses you with even more energy. In a student-led youth ministry, youth leaders become an extension of your voice to help uplift and empower the students that are in your care. While the youth pastor may be encouraging from a high level, the youth leader can encourage from the trenches. The youth pastor's vision may sow the seed, but the youth leader is the individual who waters and nurtures the seed on a regular basis, while God grows it. Without the individual sowing the seed, the growing process will not begin. Without the individual watering the seed, what was sown can easily dry out and fade away.

The level of respect a youth pastor can have for leaders will show through the stewardship and management of what leaders bring to the table, including their calendars, their experience, their opinions and their spiritual gifts.

CHAPTER 7

Students, Not Kids

A vibrant youth ministry has youth leader volunteers who partner with the youth pastor in mentoring and engaging the students. Of course, youth leaders should develop relationships with their students through small group discussions, taking their students out for ice cream, hanging out with them at the movies, or keeping in touch with the group via a group text. However, if students feel that the youth ministry is no longer relevant to them, they will disconnect. Once students stop attending youth ministry, youth leaders are left without a purpose. But even if youth leaders do a phenomenal job at building relationships with their students, it may not be enough in today's world.

The primary reason that students attend youth group is not because they are looking for another adult friend. Come to think of it, when was the last time you heard a teenager mentioning that they were looking for an adult friend to mentor them? While they may *need* a mentor, it's rare that a student is mature enough to realize that they need one, let alone intentionally seek one. Thus, while being a good friend is certainly noted and kindly appreciated by students, having another adult friend is not *the* hook a student is looking for in order to keep them tuned into youth ministry.

As mentioned earlier, today's youth are looking for relational truth. Relational truth becomes more effective for youth when it is transmitted through the vehicle of relationships. In youth ministry, relationships are built not only from the youth group conversations and consistent contact with their youth leader, but also from the behavior that the entire youth ministry program exhibits toward their students. In other words, relationships are built based on how the students are incorporated within the ministry and how they become engaged. Are they respected and treated like adults? Are they trusted to be able to handle tough topics? When addressing them or talking about them, do you or your leaders call the students "kids"? These little things may not seem like they matter, but they are the small nuances that our youth pick up on. Telling a student that they're not ready to talk about suicide or calling a 17-year-old student a "kid" can be condescending and inconsistent with the expectations that a student-led youth ministry is attempting to embody.

Students and Transparency

How you and your leaders exhibit grace to your students is an additional example. If a student messes up or confesses a sin that they committed in the past, do we try to relate to them by walking alongside them and sharing fragments of our own story (because we most likely did those same exact things)? Or, do we exhort them in a manner that makes them question their own salvation? Without vulnerability, the youth pastor or youth leader can only tell a student to stop sinning on principle alone.

Which would be more spiritually impactful for the student: to talk to a youth pastor who tells them, "Pornography is bad! Don't do it!" or to talk to a youth pastor who can look them in the eyes and say that they once experienced *exactly* what they are going through? By sharing their experience of the spiritual journey, the youth pastor is reinforcing the principle that students are collaborators and coheirs of the kingdom. Instead of telling students what to do, the ministry benefits exceedingly more when the leaders walk among the students and show the students that they are qualified to lead by example. After all, we too sin on a daily basis. Just as we exhibit a level of humility from the pulpit in adult church, any word of exhortation toward the students in a sermon must also include the youth pastor's and leaders' transparency.

We must never forget that we are all equally capable of falling, regardless of age or experience in life. The youth need to be informed that they are not alone. The typical, "I used to do that, but I don't anymore because it's wrong…" statement from the pulpit is unhelpful. Instead, a stance of comradery must go far beyond this. The students of our world go through challenging situations and cry out for someone to show them not only the "who," the "what" and the "where," but also the "why" and the "how." Instead of just saying, "I used to do that, but I don't anymore," it would also be essential to walk students through *why* and *how* you got to a point where you didn't need to do it anymore.

Since students are engaging their world through the experiences of others, giving them a sermon that includes anything less than this would be a waste of an opportunity to minister to them within their current context. Once this relational truth is communicated to the students by both the youth pastor and the youth leaders, then they will be able to connect more to the church's youth ministry and its mission.

When working inside or outside of youth ministry, transparency is a powerful tool that can empower others and encourage them to become involved. While discernment remains key to knowing what to say and how to say it, our youth need to know that you're on their side. They need to know that you will fight alongside them on the battlefield of spiritual warfare, rather than shout advice from the top of a hill a mile away. They need to know you've got their back, and that they can have your back, too, if you're willing to let them into your heart. If I went into business with a person who wanted to flip homes with me, I would surely want to know about that individual and if I can trust them. What are their habits? What does their personal life consists of? Would they bring any drama into the business? What successes and failures have they had in the past? Do they have a sense of humor so they can have fun on the job? If we were to ask these types of questions about someone we interact with on the job, how much more should we be concerned about these things when engaging someone within the context of eternity? Your youth analyze you in a similar manner and wonder if they can trust you. Until you open your door first, they will likely hold the upper hand and keep theirs tightly shut.

Appropriate transparency with students can be easily practiced by starting out within the context of a small group conversation. Here, relationships are formed through the casual conversation of asking and answering questions. However, students aren't always ready to dive into a serious conversation that tackles a major area of struggle in their lives.

In this setting, the small group leader can encourage a culture of transparency by setting the example and being the first to answer their own question. Perhaps this has a habit of working because some students in the group just didn't want to be the first one to answer. Or they may have thought of something that popped into their mind because of something you said. Or they could even have gained the confidence to say something because, "If he said/did *that*, then surely I can speak up!" For many students, the small group conversation is the starting point to help them realize that they actually have a voice, that others care for them, and that others are interested in hearing what they have to say. It starts small; but from here, a youth leader can build rapport with their students and find moments to speak into their students' lives.

Students and Spiritual Gifts

Eventually, the youth leaders and youth pastor will get to understand who their students are. This will open the door to the process of helping their students discover what their spiritual gift(s) might be. Whether it is through trial and error, or by helping them do something as simple as filling out a spiritual gift assessment, many times, this will be the first experience a student has with discovering who they are and what the Lord might be calling them to do. You can purchase some assessments or even use some basic free assessments, which can be found online.

If a student walks out of the youth ministry at the end of their senior year without ever having to lead or contribute to the youth ministry, the church has likely failed to properly equip them. Does the church truly have the right to be shocked when youth leave the church after they graduate from the youth ministry? After all, the youth are only doing for the church what they learned to do before they graduated: *nothing*.

It would essentially be the same as sending a high school graduate out into the world without teaching them how to balance a checkbook, wash their laundry or drive a car. They may be able to figure things out on their own, but it would be best to help them dodge hundreds of dollars in overdraft fees. It would be best to help them get their license while they are still at home. It would be best to help prevent them from flooding the laundry room with soap suds. If we are diligent about raising our youth in the interests of the world, then why would we ever say, "They'll figure it out" when it comes to their spiritual gifts? Too often, our youth have left the church without understanding their spiritual gifts, only to finally realize in their thirties that they can actually come back and get involved.

But why should we uplift and teach students about their spiritual gifts? Does it really matter as long as they get involved? To some degree, this is true; any involvement is certainly better than no involvement at all. But if we are working alongside students who may be more easily distracted by the obligations and temptations of the world, we are called to build up a system that sets our students up for the most success. Serving in an area that allows us to use our strongest spiritual gifts is an incredible experience. It is energizing, it is exhilarating, and we don't mind losing sleep over it. In fact, it actually gives us energy! But serving in an area that uses our weakest spiritual gifts is painful and agonizing. Such drudgery isn't how the kingdom of God is supposed to operate, for God has given each of us gifts that complement one another, just as the parts of the human body each complement one another (1 Corinthians 12).

Serving the kingdom of God could be likened to that of a fruit tree. A disciple of Christ serves others around him or her through their actions, influencing others in a powerful way. They produce fruit, and like a fruit-bearing tree, the fruit is available to be picked by others that pass through their lives. The fruit-bearing tree doesn't wait until someone walks by to begin growing fruit. A healthy tree naturally grows fruit, always. That way, when someone walks by, and is in need of what the tree can offer, they simply take from the tree. Such a tree does not have just one piece of fruit, but instead is blooming with an abundance of fruit. If there was only one piece of fruit on that tree, it would probably be quite bitter and would probably hint at the tree's lack of health.

Due to the dissatisfying experience, a passerby who comes in contact with the tree again will probably not go to that tree a second time. Similarly, a spiritually healthy disciple of Christ will naturally produce fruit without waiting for the hungry person to come along. A disciple of Christ who creates an abundance of fruit will have leftover fruit that is able to sow additional seeds into the ground and create new trees, thus multiplying the blessing that originates from them. Just as the tree can produce healthy, nutritious fruit when planted in good soil, our own ability to produce fruit of the Spirit is dependent on the surroundings we root ourselves in (our friends, our job, the Word of God, prayer time, etc.).

But for the youth, what does bearing fruit mean to them?

When someone is in need to take of fruit from their "tree," are they able to supply what is requested? For a teenager, this might look like helping their family that needs assistance in watching over the siblings, nieces or nephews; raking leaves at an elderly neighbor's house; serving at Vacation Bible School within the children's ministry; stepping up when the family experiences a medical emergency; or joining an Empower Team (See chapters nine and ten for more information on Empower Teams). Should the student not be planted in proper soil, and not produce fruit that is readily available for the taking, then being asked to step up and serve becomes a challenging experience for them. At best, the student will answer the call to serve, but it may be out of begrudged obligation instead of prayerful consideration and joy. At worst, the student feels forced to enter into a service opportunity that is not within the area of their spiritual gifts. Their bad experience impacts their outlook of what it means to serve within the church.

At this juncture, it helps to point out why a book on student-led ministry needed to go back to the beginning and explore the full picture. Without us first understanding the current youth culture, the need to respectfully address teenagers as peers, a strategy to tap into their spiritual gifts, and the requirement to build consistent relationships with them and their parents, the student may not be ready to serve others. No longer can we wash our hands of the responsibility over the youth exodus from the church (or blame the parents and/or the home environment).

Our youth are in need of the good soil of a vibrant youth ministry *now*, more than ever. Should they not be rooted in the proper soil, the dire situations in their lives will require fruit from their tree that isn't there. Perhaps this might hint as to why scientists are beginning to say that adolescence is now lasting until the late twenties. In other words, it isn't that there is a lack of enough information or tools available; perhaps instead, it is because our youth are continuously finding themselves unable to grow the fruit that is required in order to enter adulthood and be a blessing to others.

Student Involvement According to the Size of Your Youth Ministry

For small-sized youth programs that are making an effort to evolve into a student-led youth ministry, the student's role will be highly dependent on what is available on a week-to-week basis. Naturally, the smaller the youth group, the less service opportunities there are for the youth ministry. You, as the youth pastor, will need to be creative in finding opportunities for the students to become involved in. Tapping into the adult church ministries is one of the best options. Not only does this help expose the youth to the concept of the bigger church, but it also creates a low pressure commitment on you and your youth leaders. If students show up to the church-wide service event, fantastic! But if they don't, that's okay, too. The larger church body is already in attendance, regardless.

While student involvement within the youth ministry should always be active, the role of a student is more refined within a smaller student-led youth ministry. For the times that you meet as a group, involving students in your service times might be as simple as inviting a student to lead that week's devotional or asking another student to lead the group in prayer. If the group is small enough, perhaps even see if one of the students would like to host the group at their house or in their backyard for a week (with the parents' permission, of course). Since the numbers are fewer, the youth pastor has more opportunity to pour into their students and connect with each of them on a more personal basis.

Students of smaller youth ministries may have a different approach to evangelism than students of larger youth ministries. If youth leaders are not a part of the ministry yet, the charter student members that have been receiving a higher portion of mentorship from the youth pastor might have the desire to take on the role of peer leader among their newest students. Instead of focusing on numbers, the youth pastor encourages these peer leaders to build relationships with the new guests so that the love of Christ can be seen vibrantly through them. The youth group attendance may not explode overnight, so it becomes helpful to lay out the long-term goal that looks ahead at the next three to five years. By the time your youth ministry begins to grow, your charter students who are graduating may become prime candidates for your first slate of youth leaders.

For medium-sized youth programs that are beginning to exhibit signs of a student-led youth ministry, a student's role in the ministry has the opportunity to take on multiple activities. While the youth ministry might still be tapping into events hosted by the main church, the youth ministry at this stage is beginning to establish its own identity within the church. The group is also now able to start hosting and leading its own events. Although the group is still small enough to invite everyone over to the youth pastor's house, or go to the local park, it's now becoming large enough to plan these activities in advance. Friendships between the students are forming more often, and there is an active effort to spend time together outside of the formal meeting times. A consistency in meeting time and location can be established at this stage. Students may find themselves being able to focus more often on their spiritual gifts or things that they like to do in the youth ministry.

For large-sized youth programs that implement a student-led youth ministry, it is evident to the church that the students are at the forefront of their ministry. In addition to having a large share of the responsibilities for their youth services, students are oftentimes helping with events that bless the main church. If the youth service for any given week is not a full student-led service, there is at least one component to the service that is led by the students (See chapter ten for more information on full student-led services).

In the context of a larger youth ministry, there is enough opportunity to go around for all students to serve in the capacity they feel called to. Students know their spiritual gifts and they feel comfortable enough to put them on display in front of their peers under the guidance of Empower Team Leaders. In addition, a student within the youth ministry has a slightly easier time promoting a larger, more engaged community to their peers since the "fear of missing out" takes effect. Students will want to see what their peers are going to do next in the coming week's service.

The students of today's social media information age have found themselves in a state of limbo where they are not in children's ministry or adult ministry. They are also at a stage of life where their bodies are going through rapid growth. Combine all of this with the ongoing tension that occurs in the home (and other areas of their lives), where they are trying to prove to the world that they are ready to take on more responsibilities and claim their independence. If the church is unable to provide youth with an outlet for them to gain responsibility or express their perspective, the church may be doing a disservice to the spiritual growth of their teenagers. With the state of technology growing at the pace that it is, our students are experiencing things that no other generation has ever experienced before. Because they are experts in what they are experiencing, they are indeed some of the very best candidates who can minister to one another within the current season they find themselves in.

Just because students are not adults yet doesn't mean that we, as leaders, have the right to hold back or restrain the Lord from moving through our student body. Instead, let us unchain the Holy Spirit and give God permission to move powerfully through our youth in such a way that they become active, contributing members of the kingdom of God *now*.

CHAPTER 8

Parents, Not Walking Checkbooks

Traversing the tightrope of working with parents in youth ministry involves the art of balancing two distinct relationships: one in which the student trusts you, and one in which the parent trusts you. Sway too far in one direction, and you risk falling off the tightrope and losing the trust of the other party. Unless someone's safety is of concern, or there is a legal matter involved, the teenager often has an unspoken expectation that your conversations with them are kept private.

But even though the student is under your care within the youth ministry, you don't have the ability to undermine the preferences that the parent may have for their student. Of all of the dynamics that are involved in youth ministry, your relationship with the students' parents is difficult to forecast and predict. Working with parents is an area that provides new challenges and victories every day in youth ministry. Experience within the context of your particular community oftentimes becomes one of the more dependable teachers within this facet of ministry.

When it comes to working with parents, it is essential to

address communications and marketing. The larger church already addresses the challenge of promoting events and distributing resources to an adult population daily. Since many students—especially 6th through 10th grade students—are still in a stage of life where their responsibilities are few, they have not set up systems to help them remember events, deadlines and other important obligations. Thus, the successful dissemination of information within a student-led youth ministry can often rest on the communications system that the youth pastor puts in place. For example, the lead time we give in our emails to parents can make the difference between a well-attended event and a flop. Although you may have sent out a calendar for the youth ministry four months prior, changes can occur to the church calendar. Also, we cannot assume that the parent has lost or misplaced the list of scheduled events a month after they are handed the flyer.

To help organize and execute a well-attended event for the youth ministry, promotion for a given event would normally require at least three separate communications (possibly more, if it's a larger event). These three communications could look something like: the initial calendar that is sent out four months in advance; a monthly newsletter that reminds the parents of the event(s) coming up in the next month; and finally, an email communication the week of the event to tie down any last remaining details (and serve as a final reminder for those who like to live their lives one week at a time). While it is another excellent way to remind families of upcoming events, mentioning the information for your event during Sunday service announcements doesn't count toward one of these three occasions. After all, families don't sit down to plan their household's calendar in the middle of Sunday service.

By the time they grab their coffee and donut, and walk out of the door, they've already forgotten your announcement (or they've lost the flyer you've handed them when they initially walked in the door). It's not that they wanted to forget your announcement. It's just that life accelerates back to full speed once the pastor dismisses Sunday service. Too, if a family is running late that week, then there's a chance that they may not have heard about your event at all if they walked in the door after the announcements were finished.

Family budgets and calendars are often finalized by the parents. Thus, a properly planned email communications system is vital in order to ensure the successful marketing of your youth ministry events. Should your event have a registration fee associated with it, communicating these details frequently in advance will also help impact the success of your events in two ways. First, it helps families prioritize their budgets and allocate funds to your youth ministry events so that they can pay the registration fees on time. Second, it decreases the number of instances where the church finds out at the last minute that a student needs a scholarship in order to attend the event.

When we don't have a communications system in place that keeps parents in the loop, this can have negative effects. First, it can potentially create tension between the parent and their student if the parent builds the impression that their student is being negligent in communicating important youth ministry details on upcoming events. Second, it can potentially compromise the trust that the parent has in the church if the parent begins to feel like their only purpose is to be a "walking checkbook" who simply gives money on demand. Third, it can potentially impact the church's finances if parents have to unexpectedly reallocate funds from their normal tithe to the youth ministry. Fourth, it creates conflicts on the family calendar, forcing parents to choose between the church and a previously scheduled commitment outside of the church. Parents want to be prayer partners with you. They want to help intercede for their student and to help pray over the entire youth ministry. Thus, keeping them informed helps the ministry stay in alignment with the church's vision. It also helps encourage the parents to be co-ministers who work alongside you rather than in competition with you.

As long as your scheduled communications system is well established, the general flow of information toward parents should be on autopilot. While it may be manageable to conduct frequent touch points with the parents to discuss upcoming events when the youth ministry is small, the challenge of this task quickly increases as the size of your youth ministry grows. Thus, building an efficient communications system now can help toward forging a ministry that operates with hundreds of students just as smoothly as it can with five students. Unless something concerning is happening surrounding a student, or important information is needed for the church, trusting the communications system can free up your time as the youth pastor. It will help you concentrate more on the vital tasks that only you can address.

It is important for us to note that your communications system is not a replacement for the time and effort it takes to build friendships and relationships with the parents of our students. The normal flow of information should not be confused with the earnest desire to get to know the family. As the youth pastor, we are still called to walk up to the parents, shake their hands, and partner together in the spiritual growth of their children. We still pray with them, encourage them and share meals with them. The purpose of the communications system is not to be used as an excuse to stop interacting with parents. Instead, it is a tool you can use to help your in-person conversations focus on what really matters.

Oftentimes, I've found that the five or ten minutes after Sunday service is one of the most powerful windows of time to connect with parents. Not only does it give just enough time to build rapport with them, but it also makes it easier to engage in future conversations that may actually involve sensitive family matters.

Once parents know that we genuinely care about them and their household, it becomes easier to partner in building their student up in the faith. While the lines of demarcation are sometimes hard to determine if we try to divvy up responsibilities between the youth ministry and the parents, the two sides nevertheless share the same goal: to build up an independent, passionate teenage disciple of Christ who takes ownership of their own spiritual growth and who also has a vested interest in the spiritual growth of their peers.

One of these areas in particular that the two parties share is the effort to build up a healthy sense of independence within the student. While parents should certainly tackle this at home, youth pastors can supplement the process during their Bible studies or sermons by encouraging the students to accept adult-like responsibilities. Hot topics for maturing teenagers like finances, dating, social media, drugs, college, or even time management are not out of scope. Unfortunately, we cannot assume that parents are teaching their students all of the necessary life skills that encourage them, uplift them and motivate them to become independent. While making efforts to teach on these types of topics is in no way an attempt to replace the role of the parent, it can help corroborate the efforts of the parent so that maybe—just maybe—the student might actually believe that their parents know what they're talking about if someone else they respect is saying the same things.

When working with parents, one area of youth ministry that can be a challenge is the topic of driving. According to AAA, only 54% of teens are getting their license before turning 18, which means that parents are oftentimes the individuals driving the students to youth services and youth-based events. By respecting the parents' calendars through a consistent communications system, the youth pastor is able to create a partnership with the students' parents instead of vying for their students' availability. If the parents are unaware or under-informed regarding the events of the youth ministry, the family's household calendar may not make the youth ministry a priority. In addition, parents may not be available to drive their students to events and services. A way to work around this may be to ask youth leaders and students who already have their license to assist in picking up other students. Nevertheless, even with this suggestion, a proper communications system between you and your leaders would still be necessary if there is a need to connect many students to multiple drivers.

If the parents have not bought into the vision of the youth ministry, the church may be fighting an uphill battle. While it is true that a church can never please 100% of its members whenever a change is implemented, it is also true that much of the pushback can be mitigated by simply planning in advance. Making a large change within the youth ministry is like turning a boat. If the boat that you want to turn is a yacht or a cruise ship, the captain of the ship must give the boat enough time for it to safely make a turn. Based on the construction and size of the vessel, the boat is only able to turn as fast as its mechanical limitations will allow it to. Should the captain try to force the boat to turn too quickly, it may create disastrous consequences. Conversely, smaller vessels, like fishing boats, can turn much more sharply and are able to change course within a smaller length of time and span of water.

If youth pastors find that their ministry has grown to the size of a larger vessel and, yet, they are still trying to drive their ministry with the same aggressiveness as a fishing boat, complications will arise. While students can be more willing to flow with large changes in the youth ministry, parents may not be so gracious. Large alterations, such as changing the day of the youth service, the time of day that the youth meet, the rescheduling of retreat dates, or even the implementation of an Empower Team may be met with considerable resistance if the church fails to give the vessel the sufficient time it needs to safely make a turn.

Sunday service announcements, emails and newsletters sent in advance may be great resources, but they are not sufficient if the entire vision or mission of your youth ministry is undergoing a drastic shift. For seasons of greater change, this may mean that the church needs to take a Sunday sermon or a sermon series to explain what is being proposed and explain why the Lord is prompting the community to engage in this season of change. Certainly, we would not be naïve to assume that all parents will be on board. But if casting the vision, and answering questions in advance, allows more parents to understand and support your new vision of the youth ministry, you have an extra voice that is on your side who can partner with you in leading your students.

While most parents are excited for the implementation of ideas that challenge their student's spiritual growth in a positive way, there may be some parents who will pause and show concern if you engage their student on certain sensitive topics. Parents that catch wind of their student openly discussing suicide, pornography, social media addiction and bullying may be concerned that their student's comments might reflect negatively on their parenting. While it may be a natural tendency for adults to think this way, students can be refreshingly oblivious to this type of thinking. Since today's youth interpret their world through the lens of their collective experiences, the students in the audience aren't thinking about the parents of the speaker. The reason for this is because they are living life in today's youth culture, too. They know how it is. They understand that everyone's home situation can be different (even if their parents are believers).

Still, there is an element of the parents' concern that is indeed valid when discussing sensitive topics. Even though students can share some of the most powerful testimonies surrounding their spiritual struggles, we would not want to set students up for failure or create a scenario where information is shared that should not have been. The youth ministry team and the parents should guide and mentor the student through the process of speaking on such topics. For example, we would not want to create unnecessary pressure for a student to speak on a struggle that they are still walking through. Ideally, we would want the student to be far enough away from the experience to objectively speak on the matter, but still close enough to be powerfully relevant to the other students in the youth ministry. Discernment is a must, and communicating this with the student and their parents can help ease concerns (while also allowing the Spirit to move at His own pace).

Being a teenager comes with moments of lapsing judgment. Some parents may find themselves in a season where their student makes a series of bad choices. While the parent has good intentions of wanting the best for their son or daughter, and while they care so much to protect their son or daughter from being hurt, we can be encouraged that the Lord oftentimes uses a season of trials as a launching pad for their son's or daughter's future ministry. Perhaps the parents need a friendly reminder that they, too, worked out their faith and experienced a similar season when they were younger. For now, we must continue being the prayer warriors we can be for the student. By crying out to the Lord together and interceding for the troubled student, we can have faith that God will bring the student back to the faith and under the care of their loving family.

Part 3

The Implementation of a
Student-Led Youth Ministry

CHAPTER 9

Empower Teams

In chapter seven, we spoke of planting students in the proper soil to help encourage them in bearing the fruit of the Spirit that can serve and bless others around them. For all of us, true spiritual fulfillment comes when God is given glory and we are affirmed in our ability to play a part in His receiving the glory. There's no greater thing! When we experience this phenomenon, no longer do we feel lost. No longer do we feel purposelessness. We feel like we're home, and that we are exactly where we are meant to be (and doing exactly what we are created to do). As a result, faith becomes tangible. Faith is no longer simply a nice principle to live by. It becomes real when we practice it for the benefit of others. But how do we get our youth to experience this? In today's climate, this can only occur when our students get involved.

Simply put, Empower Teams are groups where students can become actively engaged in ministry by developing and utilizing their spiritual gifts for the purpose of the Kingdom, regardless of gender or age. Within the context of a youth ministry, Empower Teams encourage its students to get involved within a safe environment, thereby creating organic opportunities for mentorship to take place between youth leaders and students. Within their local and/or global community, students begin to forge a relationship with Christ through the tangible outgrowth of their faith. Many youth ministries have glimpses of Empower Teams already in place. If they have students that occasionally lead worship by bringing their guitar in, or if a student occasionally leads the group in a fun game, these churches have already begun to implement the concept that student-led youth ministry has the ability to positively impact their student population. Oftentimes, the question isn't necessarily *if* students should get more involved, but instead *how* the students can get more involved. Empower Teams help us create such a plan.

When we sit down to build a jigsaw puzzle, we oftentimes find ourselves utilizing the same strategy. Typically, we begin with the pieces that look the easiest to connect (where we are able to quickly identify and collect the pieces associated with a particular section of the puzzle). In other words, these pieces are available to us now and we won't need to dig through many of the other jigsaw pieces to find them. After filling in sections of the puzzle, the picture begins to take shape. In a section that is nearing completion, we may find ourselves noticing that one or two pieces are still hiding within the larger pile. Yet, when we are able to identify the next group of pieces that seem easiest to connect, we start another section that offers the most room for growth. Eventually, we will find the last missing piece from the previous section as we work our way through the remainder of the puzzle, but its placement was not required in order to make progress on the puzzle.

Building a student-led youth ministry that stands upon

the foundation of Empower Teams is similar. Like putting a jigsaw puzzle together, we would not need to build Empower Teams in a specific order. Instead, we first identify the students and resources that we have today and prayerfully consider which Empower Team is the best option to begin with. Additionally, there may arise opportunities to launch the next Empower Team when the previously established team isn't yet in a fully steady state. Rather than trying to draft a predetermined order to the groups that you'd like to create, perhaps the questions that need to be answered instead are: Do I have the resources and students in place to be able to implement this Empower Team *now*? Are the pieces in front of me accessible to me? Does this Empower Team represent a large portion of potential growth that is currently needed in my youth ministry? For example, it may be really helpful to have a Tech Empower Team. You may even have students who have expressed interest in running it. But, do you have the resources and does your youth ministry need it right now more than the other Empower Teams?

Whether a church has three students or three hundred, a student-led youth ministry has potential ministry opportunities for each of its students. Certain Empower Teams will commonly be needed across the majority of churches and their functions may even appear similar from church to church (such as Worship, Teaching or Tech). However, other Empower Teams will shift over the course of time and will even look and operate differently from church to church (such as Creative, Social Media or Leadership).

If you were to take a look at the list of Empower Team examples and think that a certain team is not possible or applicable to your youth ministry, it may be true for your current season. However, putting it aside for now does not mean that your church will never be able to implement the team. After all, with student growth will come individuals of spiritual giftings that will be able to take up the helm of a certain Empower Team. Additionally, prayer and sharing the vision with others can help identify those who are already in your ministry and who can perhaps answer the call. Thus, while we do not entirely wait without action, we also do not prematurely start until the resources are in place. Walking the tightrope of this journey becomes an art, and we fine tune our skill by staying in prayer, reading Scripture and engaging with our church community. In no particular order, let us explore various examples of Empower Teams that can be implemented in a student-led youth ministry.

Social Media Empower Team

First and foremost, a word for the youth pastor: It is time to admit that you are no longer an expert in social media, and you no longer will be. Gone are the days when you were at the top of your hashtag game, and fleeting will be your moments of understanding the newest social media apps and trends. While you can attempt to stay on top of your social media accounts and do *some* marketing to your students, it is only a matter of time before you will inevitably fall behind, causing you to lose focus on more vital ministry opportunities.

With students being on the frontlines of social media, they are in the midst of trending apps, hashtags, memes and videos far more quickly than the youth pastor, and any of the youth leaders, could ever be. To help fill the time, students may find themselves spending hours each day on their favorite apps if they aren't yet working. If you are the only individual who is promoting your youth ministry, you are holding yourself back. In other words, you are limited to the boundaries of your creativity, your followers and your time. In this era of clout-based networking, where the rules are constantly changing, we are woefully spinning our wheels in the mud if we're not tapping into our students' spheres of influence. With social media continuously transforming at such a rapid pace, we must acknowledge the truth that we need help in this ever-shifting climate of communication and interaction.

Instead of focusing on the exact details of how this team could be run, it might be more beneficial to simply provide a framework through which the Empower Team could operate under. In terms of creativity, content and shared responsibility among its members, this team in particular requires a high level of trust that leaders extend to students. While this wouldn't mean giving carte blanche to the students to tweet or post anything that comes across their hearts, youth leaders must submit to the reality that this is a realm where they are not the experts. Thus, this team is similar to the other Empower Teams in that a balance is to be maintained between the creativity of the students and the guidance of the leaders. With a bit of mentorship and structure, this Empower Team is able to effectively reach an extremely captive audience and create an identity that is vibrant and active outside of the church walls.

While a successful organization's social media accounts look and feel organic in many ways, the management of its social media portfolio is anything but. To be effective, the team must identify the app(s) they would like to utilize, then develop a set schedule on which to post. Since some apps have restrictions on the length of characters and/or the length of videos, it may be easier to create content that fits within the most restrictive of the social media apps. From there, the team can just publish the same video or post to all of their other social media platforms without needing to recreate any of their original work. There are even some apps that publish your content to all of your social media accounts at a future scheduled time and date.

To get started, the content publishing schedule may be aligned with the youth ministry's calendar. For example, the team could set a schedule for a weekly post the night before a youth service, a mid-week post that follows up on the teaching from last week's service, a weekly encouraging post that helps uplift the students toward the end of their week, and finally, a different kind of weekly post that switches things up (such as a sixty-second testimony or a collaboration with another Empower Team, such as a funny video from the Creative Team). To assist with consistency and formatting, it may be helpful to run all of the students' content through the Empower Team Lead(s) first to ensure that no profanity, vulgarity or distasteful content is published.

While the proposed schedule may initially seem like a lot, simply looking at any public figure or large organization on social media today portrays an active account that consistently engages the community and frequently posts content on a daily basis. If our youth are on social media every single day, and if the church wants to interact with its youth Monday through Saturday, then the church must go to where the youth are. Indeed, this area of youth ministry may very well be one of the areas of reaching the unchurched youth that has the highest potential.

Since our youth are always the experts on technology, they are the best candidates to represent the youth ministry online. The apostles went to other nations and used the language of their target audience. Just like how they lived among the individuals who they ministered to, and just like how they became all things to all people (1 Corinthians 9:19-23), the church cannot ignore social media any longer if they want to reach the unchurched youth. Your students are the digital apostles of this era. The Social Media Empower Team could arguably be one of the best evangelism tools that youth ministry has in today's world.

Hospitality Empower Team

While the high-tech culture may have been on the rise between 2004 and 2016, we are finally beginning to realize the value of high-touch relationships once again. Yet, even if we may be aware of their value, the goal of developing and nurturing sustainable relationships is elusive. Our youth are still in an awkward stage where they find it difficult to pick up a phone to talk to someone.

To put our best selves on display, we spend hours on our phones finding the perfect pose, the perfect filter and the perfect caption. And should an opportunity arise to have discourse with another individual who holds a different viewpoint to their own, a common response has evolved into showing either of the two extremes: silent passivity or unfettered intimidation. So, when the drive for social clout is high, and the culture is unforgiving to differing views, how can students find the courage to seek community? After all, making a mistake when interacting with others could be fatal to one's social standing. At best, the student is casually dismissed. At worst, they are socially ostracized through anonymous threats and cyberbullying. It is because of this landscape that the Hospitality Empower Team plays such an important role in bridging the gap between differing worldviews and the various social groups of today's youth.

When I was eighteen years old, I could eat anything I wanted. It was glorious. A fast food burger and fries before exercising? Bring it. An entire pizza during movie night? Done. An entire box of cookies? Well, you get the picture. The point is that if there was food, I stayed (tragically, this hasn't changed that much to this day). Breaking bread and eating meals together is widely known to be one of the foundational building blocks of developing relationships with others. Having food for teens is an excellent idea. Having *free food* for teens? Even better. Having free food that teens love? Now, you've captured their hearts. While food doesn't have to be served every week, eating together allows for an enriching conversation to take place and for a memorable experience to be shared. It forces the students to look up from their phones and get to know one another for who they truly are.

While food can be a component of the Hospitality Team's efforts to help develop community, it can go beyond that. If the goal of hospitality is to create a safe, open space that allows for students to feel the presence of Christ, the students that help lead this team have a certain level of freedom that very few of the other teams possess. Board games, card games, social mixers, video games and more are all ways that the group can use to celebrate others. When students show their peers how to collectively enjoy what belongs to God, building community becomes more than just a nice platitude that's said from the pulpit. When the visiting student is invited by their peers to share a game and a meal, they experience a vibrant community that really does care about them. This is especially critical for the students that may be going through a crisis or for those that who think of themselves as an outsider to the Christian faith. In regard to the LGBTQ community that today's youth are increasingly identifying with, author Rosaria Butterfield reminds us that hospitality is the language of the LGBTQ community (and that if we want to reach this community, we must make hospitality a commitment). For other students who don't have a stable life at home, or those students who are wrestling with a season of spiritual discovery, your youth group may be the only place where they feel safe.

Depending on the size of the youth ministry, the size of the youth budget, and the interests of the Hospitality Team, funding may be a potential challenge for the group. Should the team be looking for options that increase its funds, extending a weekly invitation to tithe may be a likely solution. While implementing a call to tithe in the youth ministry is a tough decision to make (and one that may need to be worked into the overall vision and roadmap of the church), it also can truly benefit the church in multiple ways. Not only does it help prepare students to establish tithing into their budgets as they move into adult church, but it also offers an opportunity for students to take more ownership of their youth ministry. When they invite their friends from school to youth group, they are inviting them to something that is a true part of their lives, both spiritually and financially. Incorporating a call to tithe within the youth ministry may require prayerful planning and careful consideration. Yet, as students feel the spiritual tug to shift their monthly budgets to accommodate the youth ministry, it is then that hospitality becomes even more heartfelt as they share their lives with their friends.

Creative Empower Team

While an understanding of creativity has traditionally been to celebrate differing viewpoints and expressions of one's faith, the postmodern interpretation of creativity in the Western world has slowly been transforming into a movement that is attempting to establish a monopoly in the marketplace of ideas. Buzzwords like "diversity" and "tolerance" are now, at times, ironic terms that take on meanings quite opposite of their original definitions (especially when a person's viewpoint is ever deemed to be counter-cultural to the popular viewpoint of the day). It is in this landscape that our youth are living in, where in order for their creativity to be celebrated, it must acknowledge that everything and anything is morally okay, as long as it doesn't impede upon the values of the others. In order for it to be socially acceptable, it must not disagree with what is trending on social media. It must fall in line with the voices that push the boundaries the furthest. Anything less than this is militaristically renounced and labeled as offensive. At best, your voice will be drowned out by individuals who have more followers and who express their viewpoint louder than yours. At worst, you will be shamed, verbally assaulted, ridiculed or possibly threatened. Today's youth have a keen awareness of this delicate situation, for they live it every day online and in their schools. But what does this mean for the church and for our youth ministry through the lens of creativity?

Creativity is a gift from God. No other lifeform on earth possesses the creative capability that humans do because we are the only ones made in the image of God. Just as God created the world and everything in it, we have been given the ability to take what has been made available to us by God and create new concepts, structures and new technologies. Not only does our mind have the ability to ponder what we can do in the future, but we also have an imagination that helps us get there. This level of creative freedom is to be celebrated, for the diversity of God's creation alone reflects this. It is here that a Creative Empower Team is able to provide an environment through which a group of students can express this God-given freedom.

With today's youth understanding now more than ever that they have the power to be content creators, the youth ministry can become a viable forum for students to share their creativity. In elementary school, we are encouraged to explore our artistic side by drawing pictures, creating a sculpture in art class, or writing a poem. However, students are no longer receiving these types of assignments in high school. Instead, the arts are seemingly placed aside within the educational system as we grow older. Through opportunities like spoken word, drama, art or poetry, a Creative Empower Team allows students to recapture the facet of their imaginations that used to be so widely celebrated when they were younger.

While the members of the Creative Empower Team can be the individuals performing or sharing their artistic talent from the stage, more youth-wide efforts can be made by the Creative Empower Team to include everyone. For example, perhaps the Creative Empower Team can set up a pumpkin carving evening during the fall or work together with the Worship Empower Team to have a multi-sensory worship experience that invites students to openly craft while the worship team plays. Perhaps the student body would take delight in the occasional "improv night" where the Creative Empower Team invites students to the stage to spontaneously act out Christian-themed scenes with goofy props. Should there be a handful of students who are exceptionally passionate about creative arts, there may even be opportunity to organize and run a student-led stage production that sells tickets and gives opportunity to raise money for the youth ministry.

An individual who is also artistic and passionate about teaching students to express themselves is an ideal candidate for Empower Team Leader. Such an individual would have the availability to coach students outside of normally scheduled services, with the likelihood of hosting drama practices, taking trips to the craft stores with students, or helping create costumes and constructing stage sets. They would be gracious enough to allow for mistakes within the creative process, but goal-oriented enough to strive for excellence. If students may be timid or restrained in the public spotlight, the leadership of this individual can help facilitate an environment that casts out nervousness or embarrassment while bringing out the very best that the students have to offer.

An effective Creative Empower Team can succeed, but not without its share of challenges. Most challenging of all will be the need to coordinate calendars among a larger number of busy students and their families. If there is a need to meet outside of a normally scheduled service, driving arrangements need to be made for a time that everyone is available. Preparation time must be taken into account, an element that is vital to consider during holiday seasons such as Thanksgiving or Christmas. Funding issues may come to the forefront if production materials or crafts are needed, which add up to costly amounts (See the section on the Hospitality Empower Team for the topic of introducing a youth ministry tithe).

In the end, however, the benefits far exceed the challenges encountered. The Creative Empower Team provides a unique opportunity in the lives of students to express their faith through a bold medium that is energetic, vibrant and in the moment. It is an area that may likely be underexplored within their lives. If established strategically, such a team will satisfy a creative hunger that the students never realized they may have had.

Leadership Empower Team

Of all the Empower Teams suggested, the Leadership Empower Team may be the most unique and hard to define. Its existence depends on multiple factors, including the size of the youth ministry, the identified spiritual gifts of your students, and the students' willingness to take on additional roles within the youth ministry. For example, in a smaller youth ministry, the youth pastor naturally gathers feedback from their students through frequent dialogue. However, as a youth ministry grows, it becomes increasingly challenging to retrieve and process feedback from each and every individual student. And while your youth leaders could be tasked to survey the student population for ideas on where the youth can (and should) go, it's possible that your leaders may be unable to successfully relay the feedback received from the youth, and vital information could get lost in translation. We must maintain a way to gather information directly from the source.

Trusting students with the concept of leading the youth ministry may be a challenging concept to envision. After all, how can we trust students who are already experiencing struggles when leading themselves? How can we ask students to advise on the direction of the entire student ministry when they themselves do not have adequate experience in making healthy decisions for their own futures? These concerns are well justified, and it might be helpful to better define the potential roles and limitations of the Leadership Empower Team.

First and foremost, the Leadership Empower Team is not a replacement for the youth pastor and youth leaders' core planning team. Not only is it important for leaders and the pastor to have an environment that allows confidential conversations regarding students, but it is also important to have a forum for youth leaders to convey their own feedback on the direction of the youth ministry. Should students be included in the regularly scheduled core planning meeting that the youth pastor hosts, the leaders may find themselves hesitant to offer honest opinions in front of any students that attend, for fear of it leaking to the student body through gossip.

Second, the Leadership Empower Team is not an Empower Team that meets as often as all the other Empower Teams. Outside of discussing what needs to be done and what can be done, there is very little ministry that transpires within the team. In fact, once the game plan is developed and agreed upon, the ministry efforts that actually touch and impact students are done primarily through the other Empower Teams. Thus, it is likely that once every two to three months will suffice. From there, the members involved with the Leadership Empower Team would be encouraged to become involved under another Empower Team that actively serves and engages other students on a regular basis. Is it a lot to ask a student to be involved with two Empower Teams? Possibly. Although let us not forget that this is the *Leadership* Team. Although some students may step forward and express their interest in joining, membership into this Empower Team is more likely to be from a personal invitation extended by the youth pastor or a member of the youth leader team.

Finally, the main purpose of the Leadership Empower Team is to help the students understand that they have a voice. But what does this look like? If we were to look back on the trends of youth ministry topics, the overall patterns hardly vary over the years. Besides relationships, drugs, sex, alcohol, social media, reading the Bible, school, family and maybe sports, what else is there to talk about with students? While this may be true from the youth pastor's perspective who has been in youth ministry for five or more years, that same viewpoint isn't held by a student who is going through your youth ministry the first and only time. By identifying students with leadership-based spiritual gifts, and inviting them to offer their perspective, it may invite the opportunity to discuss activities they like and things they dislike. This may also be the time to discuss pressing topics that are currently weighing on the hearts of your students that your leadership may not be aware of (such as suicide or drug use).

When students hear that their peers are helping to drive the direction of the youth ministry, the level of collective ownership increases over the entire youth ministry. For the student, the perception of the youth ministry shifts away from the next thing the youth pastor wants to discuss toward the anticipation of diving into the next concept that the youth movement is forging. The difference may sound subtle, but its impact is massive. Students indirectly receive validation that their voice is worth listening to. It gives them permission to keep a pulse on what is happening in their lives instead of constantly being told what to do or what book from the Bible to study. They will have an increased interest in the content of the teachings. They will be more likely to invite their friends because the youth ministry will be doing things that they know they are interested in (which, most likely, means that their friends are interested in these same topics). And finally, the exercise will begin to build their spiritual muscles in a manner that encourages them to continue being involved in the church after they graduate from high school.

Prayer Empower Team

For many students, a common battlefield of spiritual warfare is to work at developing discernment over which thoughts are of truth and which thoughts are not of truth. Similar to the movie *Inception*, the devil has a knack for planting lies in our minds, then trying to convince us that they are our own thoughts. The student may think that they're not smart, not worthy of friends, or not beautiful, but it's impossible for these thoughts to have come from God since we are made in the image of God (and God is none of these things)! Because of this, it becomes important for us to establish that these negative thoughts could have only come from the evil one.

Once our students begin to understand that the root

issue lies in the spiritual realm instead of the physical realm, our youth gain a better understanding of *why* they can engage in prayer within their current context. Naturally, the youth ministry would still help them learn to engage in intercessory prayer, meditative prayer, prayer of petition, prayer of thanksgiving and other types of prayer. However, the instructions on "how" to pray can wait until after the more foundational conversation of "why" we pray is discussed first.

For our youth that find themselves immersed within this particular area of spiritual warfare, encouraging the practice of healthy introspection from the efforts of a Prayer Empower Team can be beneficial. Indeed, there is a difference between the practice of self-ameliorating and the practice of self-examination. On one hand, self-amelioration is when a student spends hours comparing themselves to their peers, jockeying for position within the social hierarchy of high school, or editing and filtering photos of themselves to hide the imperfections that they have grown to dislike. On the other hand, self-examination is a prayerful process of introspection that meditates on what the Lord may see in us through His eyes.

Once we gain a glimpse of the Lord's perspective, it helps us see what is holding us back from pursuing a deeper relationship with Christ. While the youth pastor and youth leaders are certainly able to lead the youth ministry and its students in a session of prayer, one can't help but wonder which might inspire a student to pursue the act of self-examination more: seeing an adult praying about what the youth should do, or seeing one of their peers crying out to the Lord and asking for their fellow students to receive a breakthrough?

Versatile in its ability to meet and effectively minister to others, the Prayer Empower Team can assimilate into the youth ministry through a prayer request drop box, praying at the end of sermons, sharing a word of prophecy during the worship experience, praying over the evening events before the beginning of the service, assisting the Leadership Empower Team in the direction of the youth ministry, and more. While praying for their peers is encouraged over prayer request cards or when meeting outside of the youth service, the youth pastor and Empower Team Leader must take caution when inviting the Prayer Empower Team to pray over their peers during an altar call. Such a scenario may hinder the movement of the Spirit for various reasons.

First, students may be less willing to come to the altar for fear of being judged by the student who would receive them. Second, students on the Prayer Empower Team may not be able to keep sensitive prayer requests confidential. Third, students who are newer to the Prayer Empower Team may not be sure how to pray over a weighty situation in the moment. Fourth, it is possible that one of the Prayer Empower Team members may need prayer. Thus, it is best to leave altar calls to the youth pastor and youth leaders to minister directly to students in one-on-one scenarios.

Without an intentional effort to engage in the spiritual discipline of prayer, students will graduate from the youth ministry with the belief that prayer is only meant for unloading a list of requests onto the Lord. Rather than allowing this incorrect understanding to take hold, a youth ministry that launches a Prayer Empower Team can help its students become more successful at communicating with God within their prayer lives. Similar to a child who can pick out the voice of his or her parents within a noisy crowd, students can begin to understand what the still, small voice of the Lord sounds like within their hearts as their peers echo the passionate pleas of the student body. Should a student incorporate the practice of prayer into their lives before leaving the youth ministry, it is likely that it will drastically impact the rest of their lives as they begin to consult the Lord on school choice, career choice, spouse choice and more.

Teaching Empower Team

Within the family of Christ, there exists a wide variety of spiritual gifts that benefit the kingdom of God. Just as Paul explains in 1 Corinthians 12, each part of the body of Christ is absolutely vital. No part of the body should be expected to fulfill roles that they are not gifted to fulfill. With this principle in mind, let us make an observation that spiritual gifts typically benefit the kingdom of God through what could be considered low-volume interactions and high-volume interactions. Low-volume interactions are those that call for a smaller amount of ministry to be done for a fewer number of people (or one person), whereas high-volume interactions typically call for a condensed amount of ministry that addresses a larger number of people at one time. It is important to note that this is not speaking to the intensity level of how the Spirit moves. Instead, this is merely a generalization that categorizes spiritual giftings based on the number of individuals who are ministered to within a single interaction.

The differences between the two types are noteworthy.

Low-volume scenarios can take place over a longer period of time and there is often more grace available within these types of interactions. The art of apologetics may span years with a coworker as you slowly transform their heart each day at the water cooler. The gift of hospitality is able to gently break through the rough exteriors that someone may have over the course of multiple meals and visits. Should an individual have a slip of the tongue when communicating with a nonbeliever in a one-on-one scenario, there exists a greater chance of success in recovering lost ground since you will most likely see that person again.

In other words, a mistake in a one-on-one scenario is able to be more easily addressed than a mistake that is made in front of one thousand individuals who may not ever interact with the individual again. Thus, high-volume opportunities of ministry, such as evangelism and teaching, are to be met with a degree of preparedness and restraint that normally does not come with the daily low-volume interactions that occur more organically within our sphere of influence.

Due to the exposure and impact that it can have, the opportunity to teach in the pulpit is one of the most spiritually weighty places to conduct ministry within the church. James 3:1 says, *"Not many of you should become teachers, my fellow believers, because you know that we who teach will be judged more strictly."* Rightly so, the call to teach must not be taken lightly. Those who speak, or those who are invited to speak, must respond to the call with the utmost reverence toward the Scripture. When a speaker is introduced as a teacher, the presumption that the audience holds is that the individual has been previously qualified and is able to be trusted with conveying information in an accurate, dependable manner.

Thus, the teacher is called to respect the gravity of the situation that places them in a position of trusted leadership. Perhaps this is what James meant in his warning, for without giving the element of teaching the proper respect that is required, the spiritual growth of both the teacher and the student can be drastically impacted if the fear of the Lord is not a part of the equation. Perhaps this, too, is why youth pastors and other members of the church staff have made the mistake in assuming that students are not eligible to teach in the pulpit. For fear of placing a student into a situation that may cause them to accidentally sully the authoritative position that this high-volume ministry scenario requires, they'd rather not risk it. Instead, they have resigned to an expectation that the youth pastor is to conduct all of the teaching throughout the calendar year since it ensures good quality and consistency in teaching.

While this strategy has good intentions, this viewpoint also brings with it some negative consequences. First, it prevents students who have the spiritual gift of teaching from being able to grow it and nurture it. While not everyone is called to be a pastor of a church, many teachers are able to find satisfying fulfillment of their calling by teaching Sunday school classes, small groups, or other teaching opportunities within the church.

Second, it increases the likelihood of youth pastor burnout and will impact the quality of teaching that is delivered by the youth pastor. Sermon prep, if done with passion and a sincere desire to create content that inspires true transformation, is quite time consuming and labor intensive. To generate and maintain a quality of excellence that the youth pastor would like to deliver (while still addressing all of the other church needs they are responsible for) can become a large burden on the pastoral staff when there is no reprieve.

Third, the student body is restricted to receiving only one person's interpretation of Scripture. Simply put, the world is viewed differently from the eyes of a seventeen-year-old who experienced an upbringing that was culturally different from the youth pastor's. It is evident that the living Word of God is able to be interpreted through different lenses and perspectives. To prevent such an open market of ideas and testimonies is to set up dams that make it more difficult for the Holy Spirit to move freely.

While it is justifiable for the church to exhibit a heightened level of discernment when choosing who to invite to teach and preach, a protection of the pulpit that is too restrictive will lead to a suppression of the Spirit within the community of believers. But where is the middle ground? How can the church strike a balance between having a diverse teaching team while also having a high level of quality control over the teachings delivered from the pulpit? It is through the youth ministry where future teachers can be identified to effectively represent and communicate the Word of God in high-volume ministry opportunities. If students are given the platform to sharpen their spiritual gifts of teaching within the safe environment of a Teaching Empower Team, there is less oversight and resources spent over time as the students grow older and begin to formally represent the church during Sunday services, seminars and small groups.

Yet, even with the adult church eventually benefitting from the implementation of a Teaching Empower Team, we mustn't lose sight of the fact that the youth ministry is able to benefit in the short term from its launch today. In my experience of preaching, I've found that a message or sermon given from the pulpit can exhibit characteristics from at least one of three types of sermons: a Type-A sermon, where information is being conveyed to gather a basic understanding of the Scriptures and Christianity (*What is happening?*); a Type-B sermon, where information has been conveyed successfully enough to educate the audience on how the topic is relevant in today's world (*Why is this happening and does it fit in my world today?*); or a Type-C sermon, where lives are transformed and lifestyles are changed for the glory of God due to the presence of the Holy Spirit (*I am making changes in my life to become more Christ-like today*).

Some may be hesitant to allow youth to speak in the pulpit due to the student's lack of experience and their lack of ability to deliver Type-A sermons. Whether this may or may not be true within the current season of your youth ministry, what is true is that students are absolutely equipped to be able to craft and deliver Type-B and Type-C sermons. In fact, depending on the topic, students can be even more authoritative and experienced in the relevant issues than the youth pastor themselves!

Take the topic of dating, for example. While a 35-year-old youth pastor certainly has experience in the realm of dating, the reality is that their sermon on the do's and don'ts of dating is crafted through the lens of an individual who is married, has children, has little knowledge of today's social media, and hasn't dated since some of their students were born! If that same topic is instead addressed from the perspective of a high school senior male and a high school senior female who each share their respective experiences of Christian dating and staying pure within a high-pressure high-tech world, how much more will their students be on the edge of their seats, listening to every word? Indeed, it is the combination of information, application, and a powerful testimony of a fellow peer that strikes a chord in the hearts of youth. It makes the lesson become tangible and real to them.

Although the benefits of raising up effective teachers certainly outweigh the challenges, the church must still be wary of the roadblocks that may arise. Most apparent is the higher need for additional checkpoints within the operation of this team. For example, scheduling a student to speak should be arranged one to three months in advance. This ties back into the youth ministry working with the parents and respecting the family calendars of each household. At least two weeks in advance, the youth pastor and/or the Teaching Empower Team Leader should help the scheduled student plan and craft their message. The student is to create a first draft of the sermon and review it with the Empower Team Leader *at least* a week in advance. The student should time themselves and report back with updates on how long it takes to speak through their message. Finally, the student is to practice their content and become familiar with it in time for the scheduled speaking day.

Should a student fail to pass these checkpoints along the process, they may be sending warning signals that they are not ready for the type of high-volume ministry opportunity that teaching calls for. While this scenario is unfortunate, the Empower Team Leader must intervene and identify someone else who is able to fill the gap before the originally scheduled day (or fill it themselves). Certainly, the Empower Team Leader will explain to the student why a change in scheduling would need to take place and help the student get connected back into the youth ministry. This should not be an issue if the expectations were communicated up front. While it is true that the Empower Team Leader must be open enough to invite students into this area of ministry, they also must be protective enough to take the opportunity back from those who do not show an earnest effort toward giving it the attention that it commands. Nevertheless, whether the preparation is for a five-minute teaching or a fifteen-minute teaching, setting up a proper system can be helpful to train up your church's future leaders and properly equip them to ensure the success of your youth ministry's teachings.

Tech Empower Team

For the youth ministry of five students, a projector and microphone are not needed to reach the audience. However, for the youth ministry that has one hundred students, a projector to share the sermon's Scriptures and a microphone to amplify the speaker's voice is an absolute necessity. At what point along the way from five to one hundred students does the youth ministry require these technological resources? While the answer to that may differ from church to church, we shall assume that your youth ministry will, at some point, come to the conclusion of utilizing a Tech Empower Team and that a certain level of technological support is needed to effectively run your youth services and events.

One of the challenges that is inherent to the Tech Team is its need for dedication and commitment. In order to ensure a smooth youth service, the Tech Team arrives the earliest and stays the latest. At times, they may even arrive before the youth pastor in order to ensure that the instruments are plugged in, the sound checks are all cleared, and the projector is turned on and ready to go. To create an atmosphere where the students want to have small group discussions and hang out after service, the Tech Team may play movies, videos and music until the night's events wrap up. Depending on the size and length of a youth service or youth event, it may be considerate for the Empower Team Leader to have multiple students scheduled to assist on a given day. That way, some students can arrive to help open the church, while other members of the team can stay behind and close up shop.

Another challenging element may be that it becomes difficult to operate without a Tech Team once it is launched and incorporated into the youth ministry. Since the other Empower Teams may depend on the efficiency of technology, crucial details surrounding the planning and running of a youth service may look to the assistance of a Tech Team that runs smoothly. Should there be any surprises or unexpected failures in technology that aren't able to be quickly resolved, the downtime may impact the work and effort spent by the other Empower Teams toward the events. Thus, to help prevent disruption of the overall youth service, the leader over the Tech Empower Team is encouraged to have a well-trained list of students who are available to fill in, should the assigned student(s) not be available on their scheduled day.

One of the strengths of having a Tech Empower Team is its ability to enhance and give support to a number of other Empower Teams. With the implementation of a Tech Team, the Teaching Team is able to more clearly project their voices through the sound system and their sermons can be recorded for archival and/or social media purposes. The Welcome Team is able to create a more welcoming atmosphere when they can play music over the sound system (youth pastor-approved music, of course). The Social Media Team is able to publish more types of multimedia from the materials that the Tech Team has archived and made available (such as pictures, videos or podcasts). In addition to its live performances, the Creative Team gains access to an additional medium to distribute and display their creative works. And finally, the Worship Team can begin to make the transition from acoustic-only instruments to a worship experience that incorporates a wider array of electric instruments. Too, the Worship Team is able to more easily introduce new songs into their set lists when everyone is able to follow along with the lyrics that are made visible via the overhead projector. While all of these Empower Teams could find ways to operate without the presence of a Tech Team, the support of a Tech Team could add a layer of polish to the youth service that exhibits a standard of excellence—an expectation that more accurately prepares the youth for future ministry opportunities within the adult church.

Welcome Empower Team

The power of an invitation is not to be underestimated. We only need to briefly reflect on the fact that the incredible size of the Christian church started with one person who extended personal invitations to only twelve. Likewise, it is through the act of each student inviting their peers that youth ministry has the potential to grow just as powerfully. Yet, one thing that students sometimes guard more than their own thoughts and emotions is access to their friends.

Students will not invite their friends until they have confidence that their youth ministry will take care of the people they invite. Should they not yet be experienced enough to address the spiritual needs of others on their own, the student has to have more faith and confidence in their youth ministry than themselves in order to extend an invitation. Ideally, a student who invites their peers would be comfortable enough to say, "I'm not sure how to speak to your current situation, but you should come to my youth service tonight because I know how tonight's service can speak to that." This takes a serious amount of belief for a teenager who lives in an unforgiving post-Christian environment. There must be absolute faith that the visiting student will be loved and ministered to in a way that properly correlates with the heart of the person who invited them. It is through a Welcome Empower Team that this challenge can be addressed best.

If we host a party or gathering at our home, we make a special effort to greet each individual who walks into the door. Such an action is common courtesy. If we were to ignore our guests, they would undoubtedly walk away from the party wondering if they should have been invited at all. When students walk into your youth services and events, are they greeted warmly? Do they have someone who they can connect with? Guest students would expect a youth leader or the youth pastor to approach them, but being befriended by another student may be an experience they won't soon forget. Such an action becomes a powerful statement that reflects two key points to the new arrival: that there exists community and that there is room for them within the community. Perhaps the youth pastor can communicate these two points in a sermon. But when a fellow student embodies it in the midst of a connection-starved youth culture, the principles are spoken in volumes that cannot be surpassed.

A Welcome Empower Team intentionally makes it their goal to create an environment that fosters connection and friendship among the attending students. Striking up a conversation with the student sitting by themselves in the corner, facilitating an icebreaker with the students as they arrive for the evening, introducing one student to another who shares a common interest, or greeting students at the door as they arrive are some of the strategies that the Welcome Empower Team can use to help students feel like they belong.

Members of this Empower Team are excellent at conversation and are genuinely interested in the needs of others. They do not attempt to build friendships that appear desperate, awkward or forced. Instead, the Welcome Empower Team allows those with the spiritual gifts of helps, exhortation and hospitality to shine in a ministry where they are able to create a fun, lighthearted environment that others will want to return to.

One of the biggest challenges that a Welcome Empower Team may encounter is a need to maintain a balance that encourages friendship among the students without enabling cliques to formulate. This can be addressed in a few ways. First, the icebreakers and games that are chosen by the Welcome Empower Team can organically help break up students from their habitual formations. Second, this principle can be communicated most vividly through the members of the Welcome Empower Team. If students see the members of the Welcome Empower Team setting the example of engaging other students, they will be more encouraged to follow.

Worship Empower Team

While the adult worship leaders can arrive at a youth service, and help facilitate the presence of the Spirit through a music set, the experience becomes exponentially more powerful as students see their peers on the stage, focusing on and responding to God with their whole being. Instead of having the mindset that worship is something that they will eventually do when they grow up and go to adult church, they see living examples of what it means to be a teenager who is passionate about experiencing the presence of God right now.

Seeking and enjoying the movement of the Spirit becomes normalized and celebrated in this critical stage of life where students are constantly wary of the image they are portraying among their peers. It's okay to see adults who sing passionately and raise their hands in the middle of a worship song. But what happens when another teenager does it? Experiencing this phenomenon creates a curiosity that makes them wonder what they are missing out on.

The Worship Empower Team is organized differently than other Empower Teams in the youth ministry. While the church's worship pastor is the likely candidate to be the Empower Team Leader of the Worship Empower Team, it need not be the case as long as a knowledgeable individual is available who is passionate about investing the time to train and mentor students within the music ministry. This individual could be a veteran of the worship team, or they could be a teacher who works closely with the worship pastor and is musically adept enough to guide the students within their respective instruments.

What makes this team unique from the other Empower

Teams is the need for mentors who can speak directly to both the musical strengths and the growth areas of the students. While some of these mentors may be on the youth leader team within the youth ministry, it is likely that the worship pastor and youth pastor will need to partner in identifying individuals outside of the youth ministry who are passionate about building up the future worship leaders of the church. That being said, as the number of students grows, it is advisable to increase the number of mentors on the worship team who are also involved in the worship ministry at the church.

This offers some key benefits that are worth outlining. First, the Empower Team Leader is able to receive help in certain areas of teaching where they don't have expertise. Second, it communicates to the veterans of the church's worship ministry that they are still needed and not being replaced. Third, it shares a level of knowledge and wisdom within the music ministry that can be handed down from generation to generation. Fourth, the Empower Team Leader is able to share the responsibilities that need to be addressed in setup, breakdown, lesson plans and more.

Once students are identified and mentors are put in place, the Worship Empower Team has the unique responsibility to create its own small group that meets on a regular basis outside of the youth ministry. The frequency at which the group meets is dependent upon multiple variables and must be prayerfully considered by the Empower Team Leader and the worship mentors. For instance, are the youth at the musical level and technical level to be able to play alongside the veterans during Sunday services? How often are youth services being held where the Worship Empower Team has the opportunity to play? Are the students understanding of what it means to worship from a prayerful and scriptural standpoint? Finally, are there other opportunities on the church calendar to become involved (such as church worship nights, retreats, young adult gatherings, etc.)?

It is because of such variables that it may be necessary for the Worship Empower Team to meet more often than other Empower Teams. While the rehearsals and huddles before service may seem like great opportunities to insert training and mentorship, this method may not be able to give sufficient time for the Spirit to move through the hearts of the students who are leading worship. To help address this gap, the small group setting can help create a forum for the students to learn from veterans about the intricacies of leading worship.

Instead of just playing a song, they learn how to explore the space that the Holy Spirit is creating. Instead of being restricted to one role on the stage, they learn what it means to lead a song, to lead a set, or to direct the flow of music between songs within the set. Instead of focusing on the technical gifting that allows them to perform the song, they develop character that helps them spiritually lead the congregation through the worship experience and the movement of the Holy Spirit.

Due to the need to frequently meet with students, to teach new content, to mentor students on an ongoing basis, and to incorporate the setup and breakdown of equipment for worship, the Worship Empower Team requires a level of investment that is higher than the other Empower Teams. Nevertheless, the return on investment is equally reflective of the amount of effort that is placed into this facet of a student-led youth ministry. No longer will the worship pastor have to be concerned with recruiting new members to the worship team when they can tap into a pool of young adults who have been raised up within the church's overarching framework of worship. By properly building up, training and mentoring the youth within the Worship Empower Team, your church could effectively set up its team of worship leaders for decades to come, while giving its students a safe environment to hone their musical skills for the glory of God.

Outreach Empower Team

Of all of the suggested Empower Teams, the Outreach Empower Team was listed as the final group because of its exceptionally unique nature. Besides an occasional special project, this collection of students do not normally have an active involvement within a given youth service. Thus, students involved in this Empower Team are able to sign up and become involved with other Empower Teams that are of interest to them. While everyone is called to pitch in and assist with larger outreach projects within their community, fewer find an irresistible calling to engage in God-sized outreach goals on an ongoing basis. It is for this particular group of students that the Outreach Empower Team caters to specifically.

Since outreach opportunities can occur outside of the events of a church's youth group, the Outreach Empower Team has more freedom in deciding when to meet and how often to conduct outreach events. Depending on the community's needs, the spiritual readiness of its students, the administration skills of the Empower Team Leader, and the availability of the students' calendars, outreach events can occur as often as once a quarter, once a week, or anywhere in between. The ideal candidate for this group's Empower Team Leader has a natural tendency to know of outreach events within their community. They also have a heart that breaks for the lost and for those outside of the church.

A student-led youth ministry looks to the Outreach Empower Team to organize events or let the other students know of opportunities to serve outside the church walls. This can cover a wide breadth of possibilities, small and large. The Outreach Empower Team could schedule a day where all of the students in the youth ministry could mobilize and rake the front lawns of a local neighborhood. Members of the Outreach Empower Team could conduct monthly street evangelism at the local park or serve as point contacts for an upcoming parachurch ministry opportunity with Habitat for Humanity. Under the guidance of an experienced, passionate Empower Team Leader, perhaps the team may even have the drive to plan next year's mission trip on behalf of the youth pastor.

Partnering with local school initiatives and local government to assist with community outreach events can be another possibility. Also, there are usually students within any given youth ministry who are members of the National Honor Society and they may be looking for opportunities to fulfill their annual requirement of community service.

One of the challenges that the Outreach Empower Team may encounter is a lack of commitment from students to assist in planned outreach events. With students having calendars that fill up with school, social media, games, sports and other activities, inviting students to jump into an outreach opportunity may seem inconvenient to them at first. Indeed, there is nothing efficient about evangelism or outreach, and that is how it should be. As we clearly see throughout the Gospels, Jesus led by example in what He meant when He said to make disciples of all nations, to love our neighbors as ourselves, and to minister to the orphan and the widow. In service to others, we become a living representation of Jesus. Being the hands and feet of Jesus Christ means more than just a prayer and a quick donation. It means that we shift our schedules to make a person-to-person connection with the least of these. We engage them, love on them, serve them, pray with them, and share the good news with them.

In chapter seven, we discussed the importance of preparing our students' hearts to bear good fruit. If we do not properly prepare a good soil for which our students can thrive, our efforts to nurture them into fruit-bearing trees will take significantly more work than necessary. Such a level of effort is not sustainable for the youth pastor of today, nor is it effective. By creating a youth ministry environment that embodies a continuous outgrowth of service through the implementation of its Empower Teams, students will more naturally see where they can serve the kingdom of God and bless others. Serving the kingdom of God becomes a way of life, rather than a nice thing to do every once in a while. They will grow their spiritual fruit and have it prepared before an individual passes by who needs it. Their overflow that they had previously prepared in their heart will be freely given with joy.

Chapter 10

Coaching and Mentoring

Empower Teams

To coach the Empower Teams your youth ministry will launch, we are called to identify individuals other than the youth pastor to help lead them. While the youth pastor can help fulfill the role of Empower Team Leader in the short term, it becomes imperative to identify a different individual to lead the group in the long term. Since there will be Empower Teams that may utilize spiritual gifts not aligned with the youth pastor's primary gifts, locating the proper person who possesses the spiritual gifts that correlate the most to the Empower Team is key. By doing so, this allows the students to be effectively trained by the best leader who relates to them and can speak in a language that is aligned with how the students understand what it means to conduct ministry.

If empowerment paves the way for decentralization, adding work to the youth pastor's role is counterintuitive to the goal at hand. Even as tempting as it may be to launch a new Empower Team sooner rather than later, first pause and reflect to see if the required components are ready (including an individual who has the availability to coach and mentor the students within that particular team).

If your youth ministry has youth leaders in place who are already serving as small group leaders for breakouts by gender and/or age, identifying Empower Team Leaders may occur quite naturally. Although it would not be a requirement to appoint your existing youth leaders to be Empower Team Leaders, these individuals become the most likely candidates for multiple reasons. First, youth leaders are already passionate about youth ministry. They understand the culture of the youth. Second, they are at youth services on a regular basis. They already have rapport and relationships built with the students. Finally, they, too, are individuals within the church who are seeking additional ways to utilize their own spiritual gifts! For small-to-medium sized youth ministries, doubling up an individual to be both a small group leader and an Empower Team leader may be necessary until more volunteers assist the youth ministry. However, deep prayer, discernment, and thorough conversation must precede such a decision to extend more responsibility to the youth leader. Certainly, the youth pastor would be encouraged to conduct checkups with their leaders and continue monitoring their level of involvement to help minimize the risk of burnout.

As youth pastor, the challenge will be to maintain a student-led youth ministry model that is similar to the balanced model that was proposed in chapter three. To discourage any of the other four extreme models from surfacing, there is a need to maintain a delicate balance between allowing students to build relationships and allowing students to utilize their spiritual gifts. For example, how many weeks within a month should your students have activities and/or a small group meeting? Should any of those weeks within a given month be set aside to allow your Empower Teams to meet and discuss service opportunities for the next season? Or, if your youth ministry tends to focus more on outreach and connecting with guest students during a service, perhaps it may work well to have Empower Teams meet on a different day, in person or online. This creates space for relationships to develop with new guests, allowing youth services to be more available to the purpose of building relationships with new students.

To help the team achieve a balanced model, Empower Teams can become involved at three different levels: consistent, featured and full service. First, Empower Teams can become involved at a consistent level where there are opportunities to serve on a regular basis. These types of activities may include being on the Welcome Empower Team to greet the students who are arriving, helping oversee the sound and lights in the tech booth on a weekly basis, or keeping in rhythm with the weekly social media posts that engage with the student body. Most Empower Teams have at least one area where they can consistently assist in running the youth services. This level of involvement yields opportunity for more students to be able to help if the Empower Team Leader takes ownership in scheduling their students throughout the year.

Second, Empower Teams can step forward and commit to being a featured Empower Team for a scheduled week. These types of services would be where the consistent ministry opportunities are fulfilled, but one Empower Team receives the spotlight to bless the youth in their own way sometime during the service. This could look like the Prayer Empower Team coming to the altar and praying over the student body after one of the sermons, or a student from the Teaching Empower Team having a five-minute message in the middle of the pastor's message. It could also look like the Hospitality Empower Team hosting a special evening with conversation and a home-cooked meal for their peers to enjoy.

As youth ministries grow to a medium or large size, having a featured Empower Team can become a weekly standard. If this type of schedule is possible, it blesses the youth ministry in a powerful way for three reasons. First, it creates an eager expectancy within the student body as they learn to anticipate at least something new every week. Second, this lifts pressure off the youth pastor to attempt to be the sole source of creativity within the youth ministry (having a different featured Empower Team will naturally bring variety to the youth services). Third, it keeps the students engaged in ministry to a point where they have multiple opportunities to be involved.

Finally, Empower Teams can become involved in a full student-led service, where all Empower Teams come together in a scheduled service and coordinate any and all activities that are typically conducted within a youth service. These dates are set well in advance and promoted as special events to rally the student body. For a full student service, each Empower Team Leader communicates the theme and goals to their respective students. The youth pastor works with each of the Empower Team Leaders to ensure that all of the service's components are adequately prepared for. These events can be some of the most powerful services of the entire school year as they offer some of the best opportunities for students to invite their friends to a service. It is during these unique services that students can especially embrace their faith through the shared experience of their own peers, a vital element that is needed in today's age in order to engage with the youth culture.

Of course, not every service should be full student-led services. Such an expectation would be unrealistic and it would cause the youth ministry to drift to the High Empowerment/Low Relational extreme of the Empowerment Chart. Due to the many factors that come into play, there is no secret formula to determining the number of full student-led services that can be conducted throughout a given year. Such services could be held as infrequent as two times a year, or perhaps it may be as often as two times a quarter. A youth pastor would need to be in communication with both students and Empower Team Leaders on a regular basis to determine the level of desire that the students are willing to put on display. By sharing leadership with the family of Empower Team Leaders, and asking them for feedback, the youth pastor is able to keep a pulse on the youth ministry so that the greater team can make a decision that is properly in alignment with the spiritual readiness of the student body.

When planning out your year under a balanced student-led ministry model, it is best to consider your full student-led services as your anchors for the calendar. This requires advance planning on all accounts. First, if there is a Leadership Empower Team, it will meet to plan the direction for the next season of the church's youth ministry. Taking the information and feedback gathered from the meeting that took place with the Leadership Empower Team, the youth pastor's core planning team meets to place sermons, speakers and events on the calendar (including the full student-led services). If assistance is needed with scheduling the featured Empower Teams on a week-to-week basis, Empower Team Leaders might be able to provide insight during these particular planning meetings. Once the events and topics are confirmed for each date, the Empower Teams can take this information to their respective teams and plan accordingly.

The role of the Empower Team Leader is primarily to be that of a coach and a guide. While it would not be wrong for an Empower Team Leader to evolve into a mentor and confidante to one or more of their students, the goal would not be for an Empower Team Leader to usurp the role of a student's youth leader (the person whom they have small group with and are typically developing a relationship with).

Additionally, since Empower Teams can be co-ed, it does not hurt to communicate this expectation to the team to help prevent any confusion or improper leader-student interactions between opposite genders. For leaders who double up as youth leader and Empower Team Leader, this clarification can assist greatly in the management of their schedule by keeping them focused on whether to spend their time in relationship building with their small group or coaching their Empower Team.

Just as how the suggestions of the Leadership Empowerment Team are considered first before deciding the direction of the youth ministry, Empower Teams themselves operate in a similar manner. By beginning with the students' suggestions, it encourages the students to take ownership of their youth ministry and come to the table with creative ideas. Thus, Empower Team Leaders aren't supervisors who delegate tasks to students. Instead, the leader encourages the group by asking questions like, "Why should we do this?" or "How does this relate to the lives of our fellow students?"

In essence, the Empower Team Leader doesn't take control of the group, but they also aren't so passive that they let the group do whatever it suggests. By coaching their team of students, the Empower Team Leader ensures that the ideas and actions of the team are aligned with the overall vision and mission of the youth ministry.

Should an Empower Team lose interest or lose the resources necessary in order to keep it operational, it may be time to do some pruning. Within each of our churches, there may be stagnant ancillary ministries that should have been closed out years ago. Youth ministry is no exception to this consideration. Sacrificing quality for the sake of tradition is a dangerous move within a ministry where the congregants are only in our care for four short years. A student-led youth ministry is most powerful when the proper individuals are placed within the element that they are the most gifted in (and possess a desire and/or a calling to pursue it). While the adult ministry cannot afford to leave out certain primary ministries (such as worship or prayer), the youth ministry is in a unique position to operate successfully without the existence of any one specific Empower Team.

If the youth ministry needs assistance in an area where there isn't an active Empower Team, they have the capability of "reaching up" and tapping into resources that are typically available through the adult church. For example, an absence of a Worship Empower Team would not hold back a youth service. But, should there ever be a need to have a worship team for a special event, the youth pastor could appeal in advance to the adult worship team for support in blessing the youth for a scheduled night of worship.

Depending on the size of the youth ministry, a student-led youth ministry's Empower Teams may have small variations with regard to how they operate. Due to limited resources and/or volunteers, small-sized youth ministries may encounter the need to "reach-up" to the adult church more often than medium-to-large sized youth ministries. Some may consider this to be a roadblock; however, if looked at through a more positive lens, the scenario can instead be something to celebrate. Unlike a church plant, where the ability to pull in additional resources is limited, a small-sized youth ministry is granted the freedom to focus on what it does well, thereby allowing the Spirit to naturally build up more ministry opportunities as the students become more willing and available to engage.

The method of recruiting and incorporating new students into existing Empower Teams may also differ. While smaller youth ministries can organically phase students into the available Empower Teams as they become interested, other youth ministries may need to take a more systematic approach. Just as the adult church uses occasional "rally days" or dedicated recruitment events to funnel its larger numbers into signing up for ministries, a larger student-led youth ministry can pursue a similar method. Medium-sized youth ministries are able to fluctuate between the two methods. Under this hybrid model, not only can there be recruitment days, but the youth ministry can also utilize its small groups to build relationships with students and to discover what areas of ministry they may be passionate about.

This type of strategy for recruiting students is vital. They may need prompting to help them understand that they, too, have spiritual gifts that can bless the kingdom of God. When working with individuals who are younger in the faith, they may not be comfortable yet to point out that the church is missing something. If they are, this is a good indication of two points. First, it shows that they are developing an interest in their own spiritual growth and the spiritual growth of those around them. Second, they are passionate enough about the matter to speak up regarding the concern.

It is because of this interest that they may be the best candidate to become actively involved in the ministry that will address the need that they brought to the forefront. When this type of behavior takes place, it either means it is time to begin laying the foundation for a new Empower Team, or to bolster the support for an existing Empower Team. As the Holy Spirit is active within your life and the lives of your leaders, He is just as active within the lives of your students. While no youth pastor would disagree with this statement, it is oftentimes interpreted from the perspective of the Holy Spirit acting as an evangelist to the students, rather than a coach of their spiritual gifts.

Instead of viewing their age as a reason to disqualify our students' suggestions, prayerfully opening up our understanding of the Holy Spirit's involvement within our students' lives can help us recognize more occasions of when the Lord is moving through the ideas of the student body.

CHAPTER 11

Conclusion – Launching Tomorrow's Leaders

So, is a student-led youth ministry *truly* possible? I know it is. During my time as a youth leader and youth pastor, we implemented it at our church. Immediately, the youth ministry thrived. Each student involved themselves with an Empower Team, and of those who chose to pursue additional opportunities within the program, almost each of these more involved students eventually moved on to become a member of a young adult or an adult ministry team after graduation.

When they were given the opportunity to exhibit their spiritual gifts, students reported feeling more interested, more engaged, and more passionate about attending youth service. There was an exciting buzz among the students as they eagerly looked forward to what their fellow students were going to do next. Were the students burned out by being asked to serve each week? No. In fact, they were energized because they were serving in the area(s) in which they were gifted! With proper communication and planning by the respective Empower Team Leaders, students will know in advance what is in store for the next youth service. Thus, enough students will be in place to ensure that each ministry is sufficiently staffed by students. While this level of cohesiveness may not come to fruition overnight, I'm here to share with you that it is possible.

In a relay race, handing off the baton is one of the most important actions for the team to successfully execute. After all, if one individual drops the baton, the team has lost the race. Without a system in place that equips tomorrow's youth, the church will slowly fade or will be replaced with a church that is not adequately prepared to minister to the next generation. While elementary age students are eased into the middle school/high school ministries by default (because their parents bring them), the most critical transition is when the high schoolers migrate into the young adult age group. As previously mentioned, if high school students are not equipped and active within the church by the time they graduate, they will likely continue to do what they did in the church before graduating: *nothing*. It is crucial for the youth pastor to actively meet with the young adult minister and/or the senior pastor on individually connecting their graduating seniors to the next ministry opportunity available at the church.

This may be easier said than done, for it is no secret that the church has been having difficulty with helping their youth transition into becoming engaged adult disciples (based on the numbers of youth leaving the church). This is fascinatingly strange when we pause to think on this. After all, we go to school to get prepared for college, which is where we go to prepare for the career of our dreams. We then learn about what we will be doing for the rest of our lives, and we engage others in the same field of study. From here, we proceed to log hours as an apprentice or an intern within our field. We then become involved in a program that systematically trains us in a safe environment where it's okay to make mistakes while learning. While all of this is acceptable and expected in the secular world, do we have a school as organized and robust as those in the secular world to teach our students on how to use their spiritual gifts?

Adults must abolish the mindset that it is the youth's responsibility to take the initiative on getting involved. Certainly, after they have been invited, it is up to the student to stay involved and choose a lifestyle that exhibits the characteristics of Christ. However, this drive no longer originates within the hearts of our teens today. That may have been suitable thirty years ago when there was a cultural attraction toward Christianity. But the state of today's youth will never answer such a call if they are supposed to be the first party to act. It is not because they would not be able to deliver, but simply because today's world entices them to spend time in the areas where they know that they can excel the most.

Thus, the church of this age has the responsibility of not only helping the student discover their spiritual gifts, but also the responsibility to give them a safe environment to utilize their gifts. If successful, the student will become knowledgeable and comfortable enough in who they are and where in the kingdom they can serve. By the time that they graduate, they will have developed a worldview that puts on display the heart of a servant. They will have become acquainted with the voice of the Holy Spirit and will answer

His call to serve, regardless of where they end up after high school.

We are to encourage the youth and tell them that, no matter what anyone says, they can impact the kingdom of God (whether it's inside the church walls or outside). And while we are passionate about getting students involved, we mustn't forget that only God can reveal to a person the direction on where they are called to serve Christ—not the church. The church isn't who tells someone what to do. The church assists the student with identifying their gifting and helps them discern where they might be called. Upon this discovery, it is then that the church will guide them, equip them and mentor them. We water and nurture the seed that is sown in the heart of the student so that they will be able to weather the elements of the secular world upon graduation.

We pray in good faith that the student will develop a personal relationship with Christ through the context of the cultural application of their faith. After we celebrate their graduation from the youth ministry, we will send them off to serve within the young adult/adult ministry, or mentor them from afar if they move away to college to tap into a distant church. Will every student stay in the church? We, of course, know that such an expectation is unrealistic. However, without an intentional roadmap that guides our youth ministry into the young adult or adult church, we stand guilty in neglecting our call *"to equip His people for works of service, so that the body of Christ may be built up"* (Ephesians 4:12). Cast aside the fear of a student doing a less-than-excellent job, for you and I both have grown through our mistakes. They will, too. As mentioned before, we must not sacrifice opportunity at the altar of perfection if we are to properly build up our youth's church of tomorrow.

The average lifespan of a youth pastor is commonly recognized as two to four years. Why is this? Some may say that the youth ministry is not highly looked upon as a coveted position (or they say, "Youth ministry is a stepping stone"). Others say that the constant demand to be creative is so draining that they feel that there is nothing left to give after two years. It is a shame that each of these two arguments are posed, for neither should be true. Without a youth ministry, the church is throwing away the opportunity to raise up tomorrow's leaders.

Not only is youth ministry one of the most important ministries for a church to focus on, but the youth pastor should also never feel the burden of being the sole source of creativity within youth ministry. A student-led youth ministry addresses both of these challenges, as a mobilized student body reminds the youth pastor of their purpose and a shared sense of leadership among the Empower Team Leaders organically stimulates creativity.

Should a youth pastor move on from your church's youth ministry, it becomes critical to search for an incoming youth pastor who is aligned with a balanced student-led youth ministry model. While a student-led youth ministry can take years to build, it takes mere months to completely dismantle if there is an incoming leader who does not share the vision. To continue building an effective student-led youth ministry, prospective youth pastors must be willing to share leadership. They must be open to change and they must be patient.

For small-to medium-sized youth ministries, don't be afraid to consider bivocational candidates either. With a limited amount of time to be able to dedicate to the youth ministry, bivocational youth pastors have a natural tendency to share their leadership and practice decentralization. After all, their calendar cannot permit them to take on more than what they absolutely must do.

Be encouraged as you allow the Holy Spirit to reveal to you and your team how your church can implement a system that builds up your students in utilizing their spiritual gifts. The road may be met with optimism or resistance. However, what we do know is that the days of a single leader effectively ruling at the helm of a ministry are fading away. While it may have been able to generate results in past decades, this leadership style is no longer relevant in today's youth landscape. The church must explore a new approach. Without a system set in place that invites our students to come and serve alongside their leaders and youth pastor, it is possible that they may never properly learn how to put their faith in action before being sent out into the world as an adult.

Ministry is to be a shared partnership among the community of believers. While this mindset may be a seismic shift for some in ministry, it ironically is actually a return to our roots, as this was how Christianity operated in its first few centuries. May your youth ministry be abundantly blessed! May it move forward in boldness, and may it inspire its students to become Christ followers who outwardly live out their Christian faith. Let us be confident that the Lord will move powerfully so that the name of Jesus Christ can be heard loudly through the halls of schools, inside the homes of our communities, and within the hearts of our students. Amen.

Printed in the United States
By Bookmasters